The Final Act of God's Play

Watchman on the Wall

Tantuple Publishing Inc.

The Final Act of God's Play

 Published by Tantuple Publishing Inc., P.O. Box 1418, Driggs, Idaho 83422.

All Scripture references are to the Authorized (King James) Version of the Holy Bible, supplemented with the names of God and Jesus from the Hebraic-Roots Version Scriptures.

Printed in the United States of America

ISBN (paperback): 978-0-9983825-3-1
ISBN: (eBook): 978-0-9983825-4-8

Dedication

This book is dedicated to my co-authors, YHWH (pronounced Yahuwah, the Hebrew name of God) and Yahushua (Jesus) of the Bible who inspired the words of this book.

May this work bring glory, honor and delight to YHWH and Yahushua and comfort, peace, perspective and insight to the elect in these very troubled times.

Table of Contents

1. Introduction

This is the sequel to my Final Days of the End Times trilogy which YHWH (God) put on my heart to write based on events that have happened in the world and in my own life, since I wrote those first three books.

In Psalm 90:9-10, we are told:

> *"For all our days are passed away in thy wrath:* **we spend our years as a tale that is told**. *The days of our years are threescore and ten (70); and if by reason of strength they be fourscore (80) years, yet is their strength labour and sorrow; for it is soon cut off, and we fly away."* (Parentheticals for clarity; boldface for emphasis).

In recent days, YHWH has revealed to me how profoundly important this Bible verse is in explaining how and why our world is spinning totally out of control in almost every aspect of life and what we can expect to see in the coming days before the second coming of Yahushua (Christ) occurs. Psalm 90 is the only Psalm written by Moses, a prophet and man of God who probably spent more time with YHWH and got to know Him more intimately and personally than any other man who has ever lived with the exception of His son, Yahushua the Messiah. Recall in the Book of Exodus that Moses went up onto the top of Mt. Sinai twice for forty days and forty nights, communing with YHWH and learning His ways, thoughts and will for His people, the ancient nation of Israel of Abraham, Isaac and Jacob (Israel). Consequently, we ought to regard the words which YHWH inspired Moses to write in Psalm 90, along with the first five books of the Old Testament of the Bible, as having particular weight and revealing importance in understanding who God (YHWH) is and how He operates and has operated throughout the last 6,000 years of world history.

So what is YHWH revealing to us in this vitally important passage of scripture? He is telling us that we are all just actors on a stage for a few short years (70 to 80 years on average) and then we die and are no more. So who is YHWH and what is His role in all of this? Is he just a passive observer as we live our lives as actors on His stage, or is He a much more engaged and active participant in all of it? The theme of this entire book is that He is most definitely the latter and not at all the former.

YHWH does not package His truths in the Bible in nice, neat, organized groups of Bible verses to make it easy to understand who He is and how He operates. He wants a few of us, His people who are devoted to serving Him above all other things, to diligently seek His face and to work hard to get to know Him as He truly is and as He has revealed Himself to be for those who truly seek a genuine, intimate and personal relationship with Him:

> *"And ye shall seek me, and find me, when ye shall search for me with all your heart."* Jeremiah 29:13

> *"Blessed are they that keep his testimonies, and that seek him with the whole heart."* Psalm 119:2

> *"And they that know thy name will put their trust in thee: for thou: LORD (YHWH), hast not forsaken them that seek thee."* Psalm 9:10

> *"But without faith it is impossible to please him: for he that cometh to God (Elohim) must believe that he is, and that he is a rewarder of them that diligently seek him."* Hebrews 11:6

Thus, YHWH scatters His profound truths throughout the Bible scriptures so that we must work hard to find, meditate upon and grasp fully what He is telling us and the implications for our lives and for our direct, personal and intimate relationships with Him.

1. Introduction

Those of us who number among YHWH's born again elect are blessed to have YHWH's word, the Bible, available to us to make sense out of a life that often seems totally incoherent and without purpose or genuine meaning much of the time. And for most historians and observers of these times in which we find ourselves living, this is the missing piece of the puzzle that allows some of us to make sense out of it all.

In only four verses in the Bible, we are given the clues that YHWH has predestinated the adoption of His born again elect, in Romans 8:28-29 and 8:30-31, Ephesians 1:5 and 1:11:

> *"And we know that all things work together for good to them that love God (Eloah),* to them who are the called *according to his purpose. For whom he did foreknow,* **he also did predestinate to be conformed to the image of his Son,** *that he might be the firstborn among many brethren."* Romans 8:28-29 (Bold face added for emphasis)

> *"Moreover* **whom he did predestinate, them he also called:** *and whom he called, them he also justified (declared innocent): and whom he justified, them he also glorified (saved in heaven). What shall we say then to these things? If God (Eloah) be for us, who can be against us?"* Romans 8:30-31 (Bold face added for emphasis; parentheticals added for clarity)

> **"Having predestinated us unto the adoption of children** *by Jesus Christ (Yahushua the Messiah)* **to himself,** *according to the good pleasure of his will."* Ephesians 1:5 (Bold face added for emphasis)

> *"In whom we also have obtained an inheritance,* **being predestinated according to the purpose of him** *who worketh all things after the counsel of his own will:"* Ephesians 1:11 (Bold face added for emphasis)

According to *Noah Webster's 1828 American Dictionary of the English Language,* predestinate is defined as follows:

> "To predetermine or foreordain; to appoint or ordain beforehand by an unchangeable purpose."

Notice that it does not mean merely to foreknow, as the passage of Romans 8:28-29 makes crystal clear by using both terms in one sentence distinctly different from each other. Many charlatan false teachers and pastors try to argue this point; but they are simply trying to deceive and are not honest. The two terms mean distinctly different things and the KJV Bible employs the term predestinate four times as it pertains to YHWH's elect being chosen by YHWH since before the world began to become His own at some point during their lifetimes.

Thus, applying the metaphor that all of life is a stage and we are all merely actors on that stage, YHWH is telling us scattered throughout scripture that He has cast each and every one of us into acting roles as either heroes or villains before His play began. Nowhere is this more clearly spelled out that I know of than in Romans 9:21-24:

> *"Hath not the potter power over the clay, of the same lump to make one vessel unto honour, and another unto dishonour? What if God (Eloah), willing to shew his wrath, and to make his power known, endured with much longsuffering the vessels of wrath fitted (predestinated) unto destruction: And that he might make known the riches of his glory on the vessels of mercy, which he had afore prepared unto glory (i.e. salvation), Even us, whom he hath called, not of the Jews only, but also of the Gentiles?"* (Parentheticals added for clarity)

Thus, YHWH is telling us that as the Grand Director of His play or His story (history), He has chosen or cast each one of us into roles as his vessels of honor fitted unto His mercy (heroes) or as vessels of dishonor fitted unto His wrath and eventual, and now imminent, destruction (villains), and that as in any play, the Grand Director did this before the play began.

Then in Proverbs Chapters 16 - 21, YHWH offers us ten glimpses into His hidden hand that has been, and is, operating behind all of world history and behind every thought, person and circumstance that comes into each of our lives from birth to death. Consider this:

> *"The preparations of the heart in man, and the answer of the tongue, is from the LORD (YHWH)."* Proverbs 16:1

1. Introduction

"The LORD (YHWH) hath made all things for himself: yea, even the wicked for the day of evil." Proverbs 16:4

"A man's heart deviseth his way: but the LORD (YHWH) directeth his steps." Proverbs 16:9

"The lot is cast into the lap; but the whole disposing thereof is of the LORD (YHWH)." Proverbs 16:33

"House and riches are the inheritance of fathers: and a prudent wife is from the LORD (YHWH)." Proverbs 19:14

"There are many devices in a man's heart; nevertheless the counsel of the LORD (YHWH) that shall stand." Proverbs 19:21

"The hearing ear, and the seeing eye, the LORD (YHWH) hath made even both of them." Proverbs 20:12

"Man's goings are of the LORD (YHWH); how can a man then understand his own way?" Proverbs 20:24

"The king's heart is in the hand of the LORD (YHWH), as the rivers of water: he turneth it whithersoever he will." Proverbs 21:1

"There is no wisdom nor understanding nor counsel against the LORD (YHWH)." Proverbs 21:30

What can we conclude from this? If we are the least bit honest, with any intellectual integrity to us, we can rightly conclude that nothing is a coincidence and that YHWH is a very active participant in all our lives, for both the heroes and the villains, to shape all of world history and each one of our lives to perfectly fulfill a script which YHWH wrote long ago, every bit of which He is now directing to perfectly fulfill the many prophecies which He has left for us some two thousand years ago. As such, everything which happens, or has ever happened in the past, has all been ordained by YHWH to happen the way it did. There are no exceptions to this.

The purpose of all prophecy is to bring glory to YHWH, upon looking backwards after its perfect and complete fulfillment. And we are now living through the final days of end times Bible prophecy which, if you understand the metaphors, symbols and allegories making up Bible prophecy, you can see just how perfectly YHWH has fulfilled the vast majority of it already.

Continuing with this we are all just actors on YHWH's stage metaphor, who are the audience to this play, and will there be a cast party once the play is over? I think it is rather apparent that the angels in heaven are quite likely the audience to the Grand Director's play, who on many occasions get involved in support of the Grand Director's role to protect YHWH's people from spiritual harm against the spiritual forces of wickedness. As for whether there will be a cast party at the conclusion of this play, I think it's quite obvious from the Bible, which gives us all the outline for the more detailed script which YHWH is working off of, which we cannot see, that the vast majority of humanity who YHWH originally cast as villains, will be destroyed, and cast into eternal torment in a burning lake of fire and brimstone, as part of the conclusion to YHWH's epic story. So there will be no cast party at the conclusion to this play, although there will be a gathering of the elect (the heroes) to YHWH and Yahushua in a new heaven and new earth wherein dwelleth righteousness for all eternity which follows the conclusion to this story or play.

Having come to a greater understanding of life from this notion that we are all acting out roles predestinated for us by YHWH, in furtherance of His will and plans, and for His ultimate glory, those of us who still have our critical thinking and discernment skills can begin to arrive at some rather interesting insights and conclusions if we ask ourselves the right questions and observe people's life stories up to now.

For example, those who are reasonably affluent and comfortable today have no reason to give much thought to the things of God (YHWH). How can we know this? Because in many places throughout the Bible, those who are the heroes, and therefore of YHWH's elect, are often, if not always, viciously hated, afflicted, opposed and persecuted by the world that openly celebrates evil and exalts the wicked and the foolish. So we ought to be able to conclude that those who are affluent number among YHWH's villains, and we should expect nothing other than villainous behaviors out of them, as a result.

Similarly, those who have left a trail of broken relationships and commitments behind them are not the least bit likely to change now. Once a liar, a con man, and a fraud, always a liar, a con man and a fraud. If YHWH has cast such people into acting out such behaviors in their pasts, what basis do we have for assuming that such people are the least bit interested in or capable of altering their behaviors? In truth, the Bible tells us that we have no such basis for assuming such an unlikely thing:

> *"The wicked are estranged from the womb: they go astray as soon as they be born, speaking lies. Their poison is like the poison of a serpent: they are like the deaf adder that stoppeth her ear; Which will not hearken to the voice of charmers, charming never so wisely."* Psalm 58:3-5

In other words, once a snake, always a snake and once a villain, always a villain, no matter what their external appearance may be.

Now that we understand that nothing is a coincidence, that YHWH is orchestrating everything behind the scenes, that nothing happens outside of or contrary to YHWH's sovereign will, and given that we are so close to the climax and conclusion to this play, can we reasonably deduce what the purpose and meaning to all of life and all of world history (and thus YHWH's epic play) has been and how YHWH is likely to conclude this story very soon? I think we can arrive at some very reasonable deductions and conclusions, based on what we already ought to know, and when I use the term "we" I am referring only to YHWH's born again elect. That is the purpose of this book, using the notion that YHWH is acting in the role of Grand Director to bring about His perfectly scripted and predestinated plan for His elect that promises to bring Him profound glory, honor and praise.

As in my prior three books, you will note that I am quite intentionally referring to God as YHWH (pronounced Yahuwah) and to Jesus Christ as Yahushua the Messiah, for the same reasons which I have expounded upon in greater depth in the introductions to all three of those prior books. Simply put, the words God and LORD are titles; they are not God's name by which He has identified Himself to us in the original inspired manuscripts of scripture. The four letter Tetragrammaton YHWH is the most accurate transcription we have of the four letter Hebrew name which occurs in the place of what the KJV Bible translates into LORD. Where the word God appears in the KJV Bible, its proper Hebrew name is Eloah (singular) or Elohim (plural), depending upon the context of each Bible verse.

With respect to the name Jesus which appears in the New Testament of the KJV Bible, that too is a deliberate concealment of the Son of YHWH's true Hebrew name, which is the same as that of Joshua, namely Yahushua. In fact, the letter J did not even appear in the Hebrew alphabet until the 1500s. So our referring to YHWH's only begotten son as Jesus is an affront and an insult to both of them; and thus those of us who genuinely seek an authentic, personal and intimate relationship with the Godhead, cannot possibly do so if we persist in referring to them as written in the KJV Bible. And yet we are told repeatedly in the Old and New Testaments of the importance and power of their names. As a result, whenever I read scripture, I now replace the word LORD with the name YHWH and whenever I encounter the word or name Jesus, I replace it with Yahushua in my head and in my speech. I urge you to do the same.

In all of my Bible quotations in this book and the prior ones, I put the correct Hebrew names in parentheses after the incorrect names which appear in the KJV scripture I am quoting. I use the *Hebraic-Roots Version Scriptures,* published by the Institute for Scripture Research in South Africa, to verify that I am placing the correct names in parentheses following these placeholder names.

This notion begs the question, why would YHWH conceal His and His son's true names from us? For the same reason that YHWH has concealed the truth of almost every other aspect of life from all of humanity: to sort out and to reveal His true followers from the charlatans, con men and frauds, of whom there are many. Here's how YHWH puts it:

> *"It is the glory of God (Elohim) to conceal a thing: but the honour of kings is to search out a matter."* Proverbs 25:2

In Revelation 1:5-6, YHWH reveals who He means by kings in the above verse:

> *"And from Jesus Christ (Yahushua the Messiah), who is the faithful witness, and the first begotten of the dead, and the prince of the kings of the earth. Unto him that loved us (YHWH's elect), and washed us from our sins in his own blood,* **And hath made us kings and priests unto God (Eloah) and his Father***; to him be glory and dominion for ever and ever, Amen."* (Bold face added for emphasis; parentheticals added for clarity)

So YHWH is telling us that He routinely hides the truth from all of mankind, and then reveals His secrets to His people, His born again elect, once they are mature enough in the faith and diligently seeking to know Him as He truly is, and not as the world falsely portrays Him to be. This theme of the importance and power of names cannot be over-stated. If we claim to be seeking YHWH and Yahushua with all our hearts, and yet we do not even make the effort to know their true names by which they have revealed themselves to His people, His elect, and if we have not inconvenienced ourselves to make this adjustment in how we refer to them, our profession of faith rings hollow and disingenuous, doesn't it? We are warned in Matthew 24:24 to be on the lookout for false Christs and false prophets:

> *"For there shall arise false Christs (Messiahs), and false prophets, and shall shew great signs and wonders; insomuch that, if it were possible (thankfully, it is not), they shall deceive the very elect."* (Parentheticals added for clarity)

So who is this Jesus Christ of Latter Day Saints that the Mormons claim to worship? A careful study of the teachings of the Mormon Church reveal that this latter day cult has absconded with the false name of Yahushua and usurped it for its own deceptive and misleading purposes, and as such, is a false Christ. They are praying to a demon. The very same statement applies to virtually every other form of organized religion today, even those which claim (falsely) that they teach faithfully from the entirety of the Bible (oh really, which Bible? No exceptions? Oh really). Thus, by replacing the words LORD and Jesus with YHWH and Yahushua, we remove all ambiguity and confusion over whom we are referring and speaking to in prayer and in our speech, aren't we?

I have personally witnessed an elder of one church I participated in for 3-4 years pray publicly many times, putting the words "Lord God" at the end of every sentence of his, in a form of vain babbling and repetition, which scripture explicitly teaches against doing:

> *"But shun profane and vain babblings: for they will increase unto more ungodliness."* 2 Timothy 2:16

So he was praying to two titles of his god. Which one? I'm guessing that he was a Mason and that he was praying to the god of Freemasonry, which is Lucifer, Satan, the devil; you take your pick.

Finally, I continue to employ my pen name, Watchman on the Wall, because 1) I am seeking to avoid the limelight and drawing attention to myself, and instead am striving to point your attention to YHWH and Yahushua, who deserve all the honor, praise, glory and worship, 2) the things I teach, while the objective biblical truth, are deeply offensive to many evil and wicked people who have sought to abuse and persecute me every way you can possibly imagine, and in many ways that you cannot; I simply am not interested in exposing my personal life to such assaults, and 3) I continue to use my moniker Watchman on the Wall in my extensive Disqus blogging and YouTube replies to videos over the past five plus years, thus making it easier for you to find my other work.

Watchman on the Wall
Teton Valley, Idaho
January 5, 2021

2. The Continuing Journey of God's Prophet

In my first two books, I tell a good deal of my own life story because those stories illustrate many of the principles I teach in those books and which scripture reveals to those of us who are diligently seeking to know YHWH as He has revealed Himself to us, to please Him and to bring Him delight. I do not intend to rehash much of that material here, but for this chapter to tell a coherent story, I must take the time to summarize some of what I covered in those prior two books.

I have been reluctant to use the term prophet to describe myself because of all the negative connotations that have deliberately been attached to that label over the last several decades. However, the undeniable truth is that YHWH has called me as one of His watchmen on the wall and His messenger, or His prophet in these final days of these end times. So I will deny it no longer and my three prior books amply demonstrate that this is precisely who and what I am, walking in the footsteps of those who have gone before me, to whom I am deeply indebted. They include the Old Testament prophets Isaiah, Jeremiah, Ezekiel, Hosea and King David, among others. If you carefully study the lives of those men, as revealed in scripture, you will see that none of them had the least bit an easy or cushy life. In fact, quite the opposite has been the universal norm and my life has certainly been no exception to this; but it is rather extreme, and I'll explain why and how shortly.

I have recently characterized my life to a few friends of mine as being challenged, but blessed. I didn't use the word challenged, I used a word that is synonymous with dung or manure, but I think you get my drift. What do I mean by this? Looking back on my life now at age 66, I can see that the Grand Director of this play we are all actors in, predestinated that He would surround me with demon possessed psychopaths and pathological liars from the moment I was born, and continuing up until a few months ago when Marsha, my now ex-wife, chose to abruptly pack up her stuff and move out of my home for a second and final time. Simply put, both my mother and father, and later my younger brother, Paul (not his real name), would prove, over time, to be demon-possessed psychopaths and pathological liars, who all sought to destroy me through intense psychological abuse.

Later, I would marry my unfinished business with my mother in Barbara, my first wife, with whom I was married for 34 largely miserable years, beginning in 1979. She and I would have three children, Robert, Nathan and Megan, born in 1988, 1991 and 1993, respectively. When Megan was 19, Barbara and Megan conspired with one another to provoke me to rightful anger (not violence) that resulted in my being thrown out of my own home and barred from ever returning to it ever again, by the two of them recklessly bearing false witness against me. Simply put, I was the target of an over three decades long family conspiracy, aided and abetted by my late ex-mother-in-law, in which I was the target, the "indicated patient" and their victim that left my head reeling in shock and disbelief that a man's own family could be so wicked, vile and cruel toward a good, accomplished, honest and honorable man of God. As all of this was happening to me, the men in my life from two churches in Marin County, California, in which I had once participated, effectively excommunicated me from their men's Bible study group that I had been an integral part of for a decade. It was all a hideous nightmare that at the time I could barely believe was happening to me. Within a few months of being thrown out of my home, it became quite obvious to me that if I remained in Marin County or California, that a broad conspiracy of liars and frauds would use and abuse the legal system to see to it that I was taken out and killed.

After Barbara and Megan conspired to throw me out of my home and bear false witness against me, it was obvious that Barbara was trying to steal everything I owned and to devastate me any way she could. At that point, she had effectively left me, and in accordance with 1 Corinthians 7:15, I was free to divorce her legally, which I proceeded to do, but it took nearly 18 months to finally conclude a divorce settlement with Barbara and her demon-possessed Jewess lawyer. By then, I had been living in Idaho for over a year and had met and been dating Marsha, who I talk about in my first two books.

I had met Marsha through an online dating site in the fall of 2012. By then, I fully grasped that not only my parents were demon possessed psychopaths and tools of the devil, but that Barbara, her mother and more recently all three of my children were siding with their mother in an evil family conspiracy that was dedicated to hurting and destroying me every way they could. So I was left with no choice but to cut them off and resolve to have nothing to do with them ever again. I made the same decision regarding virtually my entire network of former friends and business associates who clearly were not the least bit supportive of me and what I was so obviously going through. So when it came to trying my hand at dating, I was seeking to meet a godly Proverbs 31 woman with whom I might have a lot in common through a shared faith in YHWH and Yahushua, and I was very upfront and clear about that. I knew full well that few women roughly my age would fit that description in our ungodly age and culture.

I tell the story in my book on spiritual warfare of some of the early challenges I had with Marsha. Three months after my divorce was final, in December 2013, Marsha and I were married before a local judge and moved in together. Then in June of 2015, Marsha's behaviors toward me became erratic, changing and frequently adversarial for no apparent reason. She began to make accusations toward me that were virtually identical to the lies that I had heard from Barbara before and I instantly recognized that I was dealing with identical demons in Marsha that were also in Barbara. Moreover, Marsha's personality was changing almost in an instant from being rebellious and defiant, to her behaving rejected, followed by her becoming jealous of any conversation I might have with any other woman. I knew enough then to know that I was dealing with some sort of multiple personality disorder, but I had never encountered anything like this before. What I did know was that it was rooted in demon spirits, some evidence of which I had observed in Marsha when we were dating during the summer of 2013. So it was not a total surprise to me. What was a surprise was that this behavioral change came upon Marsha seemingly out of the blue and appeared to be triggered by my sharing with her my outrage and anger over the evils of the 1967 attack on the USS Liberty by Israel and LBJ's and Admiral John McCain's attempts to cover it up. Why would anyone who was truly of YHWH and Yahushua object or become alarmed at such moral and righteous anger at injustice and evil? The simple answer is that if Marsha was genuinely who she claimed to be, she ought to have been supportive and encouraging of my righteous and moral stance. But she was not. In fact, she was doing just the opposite, and it annoyed and angered me to no end. She had deceived me as to who she really was.

I had asked YHWH to bring a godly Proverbs 31 woman into my life and I understood that if I asked Him, if it was in accordance with His will, He would honor my request so as to protect my broken heart from any further harm and hurt. Instead, He brought on more of it at a time when I was rereading much of my source material in preparation for writing my second book, *Spiritual Warfare in the Final Days of the End Times*. Today, I fully understand why YHWH allowed things to happen as they did, because I understand more fully His role as the Grand Director of His play and the role He had and has predestinated for me to play in it. But at the time, I did not.

In June of 2015, shortly after Marsha's behaviors became visibly erratic, and I was trying to bring some correction to her over them, Marsha abruptly decided she could no longer live with me and immediately and systematically began to pack all her things in boxes and flee from the home we were sharing. I had never encountered anything so bizarre, reckless and foolish in my life. But I knew that there was no stopping her. She was going to do what she was going to do and damn the consequences.

She had done something similar in the summer of 2013 when we were dating and we parted ways abruptly for a full three months back then, which initially caught me quite off guard. At the time, I had gone back to my books on spiritual warfare to try to make sense out of what I was encountering in Marsha, and I discovered that her constantly changing personalities were indicative of schizophrenia, that my source reference book, *Pigs in the Parlor*, by Frank and Ida Mae Hammond, indicated was the most challenging and hard to cure form of demon affliction that these very experienced authors had ever encountered. So with its reappearance, I knew precisely what I was dealing with the second time. Unless Marsha was willing to own up to her problems and willing and interested in seeking help for her affliction, I was powerless to do anything about it other than to protect myself from her harming me still further. So I divorced her, for the same reasons I had initiated my divorce from Barbara previously. She had left me, and therefore she clearly was evidencing that she was a non-believer, in spite of all her strident claims to the contrary. She was lying to me and she was lying to herself. So I had to cut her off and cut her entirely out of my life permanently to protect my good heart from further hurt and pain.

During her move out in 2015, Marsha had stolen my handgun and some of my legal documents. To add insult to injury, my younger brother Paul had heartily endorsed and encouraged her to do so which, when he admitted it to me, angered me to no end. They both tried to claim I didn't need a handgun (for my protection) and that they feared I might harm myself with it, which has always been a preposterous lie, and they both knew and know it. My brother stuck his nose in something that was none of his business, and by doing so, he was disloyal to me and betrayed me. When I brought correction to him over the phone, he hung up on me. The little creep lacked the backbone to take my fully justified rebuke like a man; he ran like the wicked fool and liar who he clearly was. I largely cut him off from all further communication since then, with a few minor exceptions where I have remained civil, but cold and distant toward him. From that point forward, I knew my brother was a lying snake who I could not trust and whom I would never trust again.

I tell the story of Marsha's and my reconciliation and my leading her through a rather extended spiritual cleansing and deliverance process in Chapter 7 of *Spiritual Warfare in the Final Days of the End Times.* I won't repeat that part of our story here. Marsha returned to the home I was leasing in December of 2015. Probably the most significant observation of that whole ordeal was that thanks to the power of YHWH's Holy Spirit working in and through me, I was able to genuinely forgive Marsha for the incredible cruelty and callousness with which she had left me and had then borne false witness against me, claiming that she was afraid for her safety because of me and had sought a restraining order against me, which she knew was a monstrous lie that hit every hot button imaginable of mine after what my first wife Barbara and my daughter Megan had done to me back in California three years earlier, none of which was even remotely true. I found it equally incredible and callous that of the church community of people she used to help her move all her stuff out of the home we shared about ten days after she packed her things and fled, not one of them spoke to me or even bothered to look me in the eyes. Their profession of being followers of Christ was not the least bit matched by any evidence of compassion or caring on their part. I was truly appalled, but not the least bit surprised, because I was already fully onto the con and fraud of all forms of organized religion by that point.

When Marsha left, I was largely abandoned and alone, and I turned to the only source of solace and comfort I had, deepening my relationship with YHWH and Yahuwah. In particular, I resolved to observe the sabbath, as the Bible teaches, and to do no labor on Saturday, the seventh day of the week. I prepared my meals the day before so I would not have to cook on the sabbath, and I used the time to read from the

Book of Psalms, either the first or the last 75 psalms every sabbath day. I continue to do this today. I found that by doing so, it calms my spirit and causes me to grow closer to Father YHWH, and He to me, and anchors my spirit for the following week.

Once Marsha and I reconciled and she returned to live with me, we lived together as biblical husband and wife for the next five years. The Bible make no reference to any form of a legal contract, marriage license or ceremony before a priest, pastor or judge for a man and a woman to be married. They strictly have to make a lifelong covenant and commitment to live harmoniously with one another and to consummate their union by coming together in physical intimacy. After two contentious divorces, I was not the least bit interested in exposing myself to those legal and financial risks ever again. So we never legally remarried with a marriage license and defacto legal marriage contract.

In late August of this year, Marsha went on a four day girls' camping trip with her vintage trailer and I had a bit more time on my hands at night to think and reflect over the four day weekend. It dawned on me that Marsha's and my intimacy together was being seriously neglected and that it was not the least bit attributable to a lack of interest on my part; but it was on her part. So I went to my bookshelves and pulled out four books on the subject (I have a number of them from my prior marriage challenges) and flipped through them to remind myself of some of their teachings and thoughts on the subject. These were the four books:

> *How to Make Love to the Same Person for the Rest of Your Life and Still Love It,* by Dagmar O'Connor
>
> *The Proper Care & Feeding of Husbands,* by Dr. Laura Schlessinger
>
> *The Five Love Languages,* by Gary Chapman
>
> *Love Life for Every Married Couple,* by Ed Wheat, M.D.

As I flipped through them, I was reminded of the following two passages in the Bible and I went back to read them once again:

> *"Let the husband render unto the wife due benevolence: and likewise also the wife unto the husband. The wife hath not power of her own body, but the husband, and likewise also the husband hath not power of his own body, but the wife. Defraud ye not one another, except it be with consent for a time, that ye may give yourselves to fasting and prayer; and come together again, that Satan tempt you not for your incontinency."* 1 Corinthians 7:3-5

> *"Nevertheless let every one of you in particular so love his wife even as himself; and the wife see that she reverence her husband."* Ephesians 5:33

So these passages are telling husbands and wives who are striving to do YHWH's will how to effectively engage with one another in marriage so that there will be harmony and so each partner's core needs will be met. In the case of the Ephesians 5:33 passage, the word reverence means fear mingled with respect, esteem and affection. Given all I have done for Marsha, and given who I so clearly am in every respect, it was painfully obvious to me that I deserved reverence from Marsha and that part of such reverence ought to be her being responsive to and interested in engaging in physical intimacy with me, but neither of those things were happening.

So I set aside the four books and waited for Marsha to return home from her girls' camping trip. Over the next week or so, I began to broach these subjects with Marsha and I got a decidedly guarded, if not an adversarial and hostile response from her, which really annoyed me. I asked her to look through the four books I had left out for her to look at. She protested that she was not much of a reader. Then she corrected herself and said, "Except for the Bible." I was not the least bit convinced. I even read her the above two passages in the Bible so that she would be without excuse and know what they say. She was not moved in the least by this, nor did she show the least bit of interest in considering that she might be in error and thoughtless and unkind toward me.

A few nights later, she told me that she had skimmed the four books I had left out for her. The fact that she merely skimmed them told me that she was not the least bit receptive to any of their messages, and that alone was both irritating and insulting to me. She then proceeded to tell me that the first book was demonic and she had nothing but scorn to direct at Dr. Laura Schlessinger and her book, probably because of its title. That was it. I had had it with Marsha and rolled away from her in bed. She came over to put her hand on my shoulder and told me that she loved me. No, she did not. It was all a monstrous con and now I knew. I said nothing. She rolled away shortly thereafter. She then knew that I knew. The next morning we had a brief argument before I went off to work in which she was talking erratically and inconsistently and her demons accused me of some of the same lies, in virtually the same words, which Barbara's demons had falsely accused me of years before. I really wasn't interested in getting drawn into her and her demons' drama and left our condo to go to work.

I got home around 7:30 p.m. to a dark house and piles of packed cardboard boxes of Marsha's things in my living room. She had left me a text message telling me that it was late and she would be staying overnight in Idaho Falls some 75 miles away from our home. Really nice touch, don't you think? Full of compassion, kindness and consideration for the other person, don't you think? This was the very same stunt that Marsha had pulled on me five years earlier, for which she had later confessed and repented, and yet she was doing it to me yet again! It was heartless, cruel and deliberately brutal on her part. So apparently the whole prior five years of our marriage was a sham, a con job and a lie. I was totally done with her. I just wanted her out of my life completely and forever, as fast as I could enable it to happen.

My first concern was to protect myself against her stealing any of my valuables again. She had demonstrated previously that she had no hesitancy to steal from me when she left the first time; I had no reason to believe that she would not steal from me again, and I could not afford to take the chance that she might. I immediately opened a safe deposit box with a local bank and secured my precious metal coins and handgun in it and closed my bank checking account that Marsha was able to access and opened a new one without her name on it. I then sent her a text and asked her to meet me at home so we could talk some things through. I told her directly that it was best for both of us that she was leaving, but that we didn't have to do this acrimoniously. We could and ought to be civil, kind and respectful toward each other as mature adults as we parted ways. I told her what I had done and explained that I had access to her checking account and that we should both go into our bank and sign paperwork to remove my name from her checking account. I also asked her to show me some kindness and compassion as she moved out and to not leave me desolate as she had done the prior time. I asked her to leave me some of her quilts for bedding and I asked her to allow me to care for Matti, our 13 year old female Maltese-Yorkshire terrier whom I adore, and she adores me, which Marsha fully knows. Somewhat to my pleasant surprise, she agreed to both of my requests.

Over the next ten days, Marsha secured an apartment in Idaho Falls where she grew up and where she still has family and I agreed to help her pack a U-Haul truck and drive it to Idaho Falls for her. The separation of our things was amicable and collaborative. YHWH's Holy Spirit was all over me throughout that entire time. I had a goal: get Marsha completely out of my life as smoothly and as swiftly as possible. Forever. Do whatever it took to achieve that goal. And I did. YHWH protected my heart and I felt very little emotion after the first day or so.

What Marsha chose to do was reckless, irresponsible and very foolish. Her assets are very modest, so she is going to have to find some part time work to cover her monthly bills. When she was living with me, I covered all of our living expenses. But I also knew that YHWH, the Grand Director, was orchestrating all of this behind the scenes, and that Marsha was in the process of destroying herself by her foolish, callous and reckless actions. Marsha had conned herself and conned me into believing that she is one of God's elect, but God is never conned. He knew all along. I have long suspected that Marsha might not be all she claimed to be, but I figured that I would find out one way or the other when and if the time came. Now I know. And I'm at peace with it.

On the day we moved Marsha, we packed the U-Haul truck and trailer early in the morning and I drove them to Marsha's new apartment in Idaho Falls, where a number of her family members met us to unload her things. I was totally focused on the goal. I felt nothing. That was God shielding my heart. We then returned in my car to Teton Valley where Marsha's Jeep was waiting with more stuff packed in it. She reminded me that she had asked if I would write her a check for some funds to cover the costs of her move and her first month of expenses. I had reluctantly agreed to do so, although I found it highly audacious and brazen on her part to even consider asking such a thing from me after what she was putting me through. It was as if she was adding insult to injury. But I had my goal. So I had reluctantly agreed. I wrote her a check for $1,000 and gave it to her and walked her out to her Jeep and she left to return to her new apartment in Idaho Falls. That was Saturday, September 19.

Early on the morning of Sunday, September 20, YHWH woke me up to reveal to me that the check I had written to Marsha the day before was written on a check from my old checking account which I had closed ten days before. My new checks had arrived on Friday afternoon as we were picking up the U-Haul truck and grabbing some dinner, and so I never got around to putting the checks for the new checking account in my check book. The first thing that occurred to me was, Oh crap, now I have to write out another check to Marsha and drive it down to Idaho Falls on Sunday, when I'm dog tired, and leave the check in her mailbox or a crack in her apartment door, because I in no way wished to see or talk to her ever again.

But then YHWH, the Grand Director of this play, reminded me that even though I had forgotten these things, He had not.

Had He wanted me to write Marsha a check from the new checking account, He could have easily brought it to my awareness the day before. But He did not; quite intentionally. So because of my deeper understanding of how active God is in my life and in all our lives, I was able to deduce and see that YHWH did not want Marsha to have access to any more of my funds. He had allowed her to brazenly ask me to write her a check the day before, and He had caused me to only reluctantly agree to it, with considerable irritation, which I did not reveal to Marsha. But YHWH knew, because He influences my thoughts constantly. He was the ultimate source of my feeling annoyed by Marsha's unjustified, callous and immoral request of me.

So I sent a text message to Marsha and asked her not to try to cash the check that I had given her that would not clear and that God had revealed this to me through His waking me up at 2 a.m. in the morning to point this out to me and that He clearly did not want her to have access to those funds and so I asked her to leave it at that. Her demons replied shortly thereafter, accusing me of lying and deliberately defrauding her. That did it. I blocked her and removed her as a contact on my phone. I will not tolerate her and her demons abusing me and accusing me of anything I did not do ever again. I am totally through with her and her evil.

Early the next morning, again at around 2 a.m., YHWH took me in the spirit to the third heaven, just as He did with the Apostle Paul that he describes in 2 Corinthians 12:2-9:

> *"I knew a man in Christ (the Messiah) above fourteen years ago, (whether in the body, I cannot tell; or whether out of the body I cannot tell: God (Eloah) knoweth;) such an one caught up to the third heaven. And I knew such a man, (whether in the body, or out of the body, I cannot tell: God (Eloah) knoweth;) How that he was caught up into paradise, and heard unspeakable words, which is not lawful for a man to utter. Of such an one will I glory: yet of myself I will not glory, but in mine infirmities. For though I would desire to glory, I shall not be a fool; for I will say the truth: but now I forbear, lest any man should think of me above that which he seeth me to be,*

> *lest I should be exalted above measure. For this thing I besought the Lord thrice, that it might depart from me. And he said unto me, My grace is sufficient for thee: for my strength is made perfect in weakness. Most gladly therefore will I rather glory in my infirmities, that the power of Christ (the Messiah) may rest upon me."*

This infirmity that Paul spoke of was apparently some form of significant visual impairment that forced Paul to dictate all his epistles with the help of a scribe, because he could barely see. But YHWH clearly showed Paul some truly marvelous things in the third heaven that inspired Paul and gave him unspeakable joy and hope.

In my own case, I had three visions early in the morning of Monday, September 21. In the first one, I was in the new heaven and new earth wherein dwelleth righteousness and I was a king of major royalty in a palace with a large Roman bath of some sort. I was unclothed with a drape over me and was being attended to by a number of beautiful young women who were also unclothed and attending to my every sensual pleasure and delight. I was beside myself with unspeakable joy!

In the second vision, I was sitting on my throne and my people were coming to me with requests for help or decisions from me of some kind. I was reminded of King Ahasuerus in the Book of Esther and his queen, Vashti, who refused to heed his request to join him and his nobles at a feast that the king was hosting for his nobles and princes, and how his lords advised him to banish Queen Vashti and to replace her with another maiden who would please the king to send a clear message to all wives in the empire of 127 provinces that every man should bear rule in his own house. I was further recalling how Esther and the other maidens spent a year purifying themselves before they went into the king to please and delight him as they auditioned for the role of his new queen. Esther did just that, and she obtained grace and favor in his sight and he made her his queen in the place of Vashti. She clearly was wise enough to know her role and response to the king and obey God, and God blessed her for it. Later in the story of Esther, she is only able to approach the king when and if he summons her to approach him. Esther showed reverence and profound respect toward the king, as any wise and godly wife ought to show to her husband, and the king rewarded her accordingly. I was distinctly aware that the king's insistence on absolute respect being shown to him that was essential for him to enjoy and exercise the authority he required to be truly effective as a king. This is in sharp contrast to the experience I have endured at the hands of my two foolish and ungodly ex-wives.

The third event was more of a revelation from God than a vision. YHWH informed me that the next day, Tuesday, September 22, would be THAT DAY: the day of Yahushua's second coming. I was ecstatic! The visions which YHWH had given me were so marvelous and so beyond my wildest imaginings that I was filled with unspeakable joy. Now all of the suffering and all of the experiences I have had, and the wisdom I have acquired from them, make coherent sense out of my troubled life.

On the following morning, Tuesday, September 22, I got up and barbecued the last of some kippered herrings I had for breakfast, along with some scrambled eggs. My brother Paul had sent the herrings to me as a gift earlier in the summer, apparently as a gesture of goodwill to perhaps remind me of a good memory of mine growing up in our parents' home. Sadly, I have no such fond memories. It was an awful time in my life. But out of respect for my younger brother and his apparent gesture of goodwill (which he owed me), I cooked the last of the kippered herrings and began to eat them for breakfast when YHWH put it on my heart to write a text message along the following lines to my brother:

> "Do you remember that morning in February of 2011 over breakfast at the Pacific Cafe in which I told you that I expected to be part of the gathering to Christ sometime soon, and how you angrily stood up and rudely and abruptly stormed out of the restaurant, making quite a scene? Well today is THAT DAY.

> By this evening, I expect to be with God and Christ in heaven where I have longed to be these many years. Good-bye."

About two hours later, as I was walking by my office window, I noticed two sheriff SUVs parked on our shared complex driveway. I assumed that their presence must be related to me, so I went to my chair in my living room, sat down and waited. Within about five minutes, two sheriff's deputies walked down the sidewalk next to my living room window to the corner, checked the unit number, came back to my front door and knocked. Here is roughly how the conversation went:

> "Good morning officers, how can I help you?"
>
> "Are you Watchman on the Wall?"
>
> "I am."
>
> "Is everything OK? Are you anxious or having suicidal thoughts? We recently received a call from your brother expressing concern that you may be suicidal or trying to take your own life."
>
> I almost burst out laughing, but out of respect for the officers, who were dead serious, I said,
>
> "No officers, not only am I OK, I am filled with unspeakable joy because today is the day of Christ's second coming and I am going to be going home to be with him today. My brother hates God and hates me and this is how he responded to the text I sent him just a few hours ago. Here is the text message I sent to my brother that led to his placing a call to your office." I then handed my phone to one of the two deputies who read the text and handed it back to me.
>
> I continued, very calmly, "Gentlemen, you probably don't know who I am, but I am a biblical Christian and a published author of three rather remarkable books concerning the global conspiracy and its many obvious links to the fulfillment of end times Bible prophecy. So this is my field of expertise. Those

> books are sitting over there on my reading table next to my chair, would you like to see them?" They declined my offer.
>
> At about this point, the second deputy told me that they had just received another emergency call that they needed to attend to and they started backing away from my door. I wasn't convinced. I think they were frightened by what I was telling them, because they knew that they were not right with God. I was reminded of this verse in the Book of Psalms:
>
> *"For lo, the kings were assembled, they passed by together. They saw it (the palace of God in heaven), and so they marvelled; they were troubled, and hasted away. Fear took hold upon them there, and pain, as a woman in travail."* Psalm 48:4-6
>
> Those deputies were hastening away in fear, and I knew it, and I felt sorry for them.

Shortly thereafter, a friend of mine on Facebook who lives in Poland informed me that Marsha had just contacted him via Facebook Messenger trying to discredit me and encouraging him to abandon any continuing communication with me. I knew that Marsha was planning on returning to Teton Valley that day for a doctor's appointment. She had texted me that she wanted to drop by some household items of mine she had, but I asked her not to. I told her that it was just meaningless stuff anyway and that I neither wished to see or speak to her again, so I thought it best that she not stop by. YHWH revealed to me in my thoughts that my brother Paul and Marsha had been scheming and colluding with one another over the past five years (hidden from me) to seek to harm me in some way. All the while, for five years under my roof, generously financed entirely by me, Marsha had been enjoying my generosity, attention and kindnesses, which were many, including a number of nice vacations together and many meals out.

The depths of the duplicity, deception, treachery, betrayal and depravity that Marsha was obviously capable of defies words. It is unspeakable evil with which few people have ever had to endure at the hands of another. And as YHWH revealed to me, apparently my brother was fully in on the treachery and betrayal. My friend Jake and I deduced that while she was back in the Valley, it was likely she had a dual purpose and that her second purpose was to try to discredit me any way she could and try to convince anyone we knew in common that I was out of my mind. It's a very common gaslighting trick and ploy of those who are pure evil. The goal is to isolate their victims socially as much as they can, and try to make them think that they are losing their minds.

Yahushua's second coming obviously did not happen that day, as YHWH had told me, and as the sun began to set I began to wonder why He had misled me. I felt inspired to go on Facebook and tell this story of what was happening to me to those following me and to try to make sense out of this. A day later, I figured it out. YHWH used me to trust Him so I would have reason to write the text message that I did to my brother, which trapped him and led him to foolishly reveal the depths of his own profound ignorance, duplicity and his hatred for God and anything related to the Bible. I already knew that Paul was an ignorant, God-hating fool, but when he acted on my text message the way he did, he unwittingly and fully exposed himself for who he has always been. Until that day, I never fully grasped that my younger brother was perhaps more demon-possessed and more of a hateful liar than even our two parents were. So, including my first wife's late mother who was the ring leader of my first marriage's family conspiracy, my life has been defiled and assaulted by nine demon-possessed psychopaths, pathological liars and tools of the devil, which begs the question, why me?!?

I have long been saying and writing on social media that I am the devil's worst nightmare, and I sincerely mean that. I hate the devil with every ounce of my being for the profound pain and cruelty that he has brought me my entire life. He began messing with me from the moment I was born and he has never let up. Why? I now think it's obvious: because he knew how dangerous I was and who I would one day become. I am now that man who the devil rightly fears because of who I am.

Yes, I am an adopted son of the Living God, YHWH. But I am much more than that: I am His watchman on the wall, His prophet and major royalty in the kingdom of God soon to come. The contents of my first three books prove this claim conclusively for anyone with YHWH's Holy Spirit living in them. Those three books of mine are so damaging to the schemes of the devil, that he is filled with uncontrollable rage over them, and he has been devoted to taking every shot he could to hurt me and to destroy me if he could. But he cannot; because YHWH won't let him.

I wrote a rather lengthy thought piece on my Facebook timeline that night that took me seven hours to compose from 5 p.m. to midnight. I knew I was under an intense demonic attack the entire time I was writing it. I could feel it in my body, manifesting as some sort of vibrational energy. I had trouble focusing my eyes on my computer screen, and my keyboard was producing an endless string of typos; far more than is usual for me. But I sensed that YHWH was calling me to be dogged and tenacious and see it through to a clean thought piece and to post it, which I finally did.

However, the demonic oppression did not subside. I tried to go to bed, but could not get comfortable to sleep. I recalled how five years earlier, shortly after Marsha had left me the first time, I experienced much the same vibrational energy that was leaving me exhausted late at night. At first, I prayed to YHWH asking Him to remove it so I could go to sleep and get some much-needed rest, but nothing happened. So after about an hour and a half of struggling to go to sleep, I got up out of bed and located and pulled down every home furnishing that had belonged to Marsha and piled them on the coffee table in my living room. Down came window valences which Marsha had sewn and hung, framed pictures of the two of us, a number of vintage decorations sitting on the top of my kitchen cabinets, a wall mirror screwed into the wall of one of the bedrooms, other framed pictures that Marsha had bought at a local second hand store which had no meaning to me, some decorative candles, candle holders and vintage soap dishes. I pulled on my clothes and hauled all that stuff outside to the community dumpster and threw them away at 2 a.m. in the morning. When I got back inside, the demonic oppression was gone and I went to bed and fell asleep utterly exhausted.

Upon waking on Wednesday morning, I perceived that YHWH had tread down my enemies, those of witchcraft, the occult, Satanists and New Agers who live in my Valley, whom Marsha appeared to have enlisted as allies of hers to direct their curses, spells and incantations in my direction the day and night before. Later that day, at 4:55 p.m., the wife of a friend of mine sent me a text asking if I was available to talk to her. YHWH inspired me to reply telling her no, that I would only make myself available to her if my friend and her husband, was part of it. About 48 hours later, I discovered that Vicki, my friend's wife, had been subjected to a demonic verbal attack three times over the public radio system on our local school district's school buses by another woman driver, which were overheard by every school student and bus driver during the afternoon school bus routes. The woman bus driver who verbally accosted Vicki should have been fired on the spot for her outrageous conduct, but she was not.

On Friday September 25, an envelope came to my post office box with a return address from Marsha on it. I opened it while I was on the phone in the grocery store parking lot with my friends Rich and Vicki, hearing about the demonic attack Vicki had been subjected to over the school bus system radio at the hands of another woman driver two days before. Inside the envelope from Marsha was the check I had written to her on my old, closed checking account. It struck me then that Vicki had been demonically attacked the day after I had endured my own demonic affliction and that it was probably no coincidence that something similar happened to Vicki the following day. Marsha knew of my friendship with Rich and Vicki and she may very well have had some hand in instigating some form of demonic attack on my friends to further isolate me. I certainly knew that the way to mess with Rich would be to mess with Vicki.

The returned check from Marsha was postmarked Wednesday, September 23 at 2 p.m. from Idaho Falls. There was no reason for her to return the check to me; she could have just torn it up and thrown it away. But YHWH inspired her to return it to me for some reason. Given the timing of when Marsha mailed it, I suspect it was YHWH signaling to me that the victory was ours and that the forces of darkness in Teton Valley, Idaho had been seriously thrashed the night before. In a way, it was Marsha's and her demons' way of conceding defeat to me, although I'm sure she and they do not perceive it that way. But I suspect YHWH does, and He is the one who counts.

I used that Friday to vacuum, mop and clean my entire condo from top to bottom and to remove any last vestiges of Marsha's having lived there. It was yet another level of cleansing my home from demon spirit influences and presences. When I was done, I anointed the door posts and lintels of each of the four outside doors of my condo with olive oil, breaking all curses, spells, hexes and vexes that had been sent upon me or my home and then binding and casting out any remaining demons attached to those just broken curses, hexes, vexes and spells before I closed and sealed the fourth doorway, as I teach in my book, *Spiritual Warfare in the Final Days of the End Times.* My sabbath day the following day (Saturday) was peaceful, tranquil and serene: just the way I like it to be. Sometime during this first week that Marsha was gone from my home, I asked YHWH if He would allow me to bring my KJV Bible and my little dog Matti with me when His son Yahushua returns in His second coming to gather we, the elect, to Himself in the clouds. I had and have the distinct sense that YHWH is going to allow me these two blessings. But only time will tell.

The following day, Sunday, September 26, I recognized that I really needed to replace the quilts, bedspread and apron on my bed to rid my home of literally everything of Marsha's and to replace several vintage items of hers I had thrown out five days earlier in my purge of her things early in the morning. So I drove over the pass to Jackson, WY to try to find replacement bedding, but the store I knew of over there, TJ Maxx, was completely picked over and had nothing that I was looking for. But on the way over the mountain pass to Jackson, the fall leaves of the aspen trees were bright, vibrant yellow, the most beautiful I think I've ever seen, and I could not help but shout out in glee and delight at the beauty of those fall colors. I had the very distinct sense that YHWH had inspired my trip to Jackson, and sort of said to me, "Come on son, let's go for a ride in the country this afternoon," just so He could share the wonders and beauty of His creation with me after a long and exhausting week. I felt truly blessed and I was.

Additionally, on the trip over to Jackson, YHWH inspired my thoughts to reflect on the visions of the third heaven that He had imparted to me on Monday morning, especially my kingship and the notion that I am destined by YHWH to enjoy a harem of beautiful, giving and reverential woman attending to my sensual pleasures forever. He reminded me of a scene I had encountered on my bus driving work for the rafting industry in Jackson about a month before in which my passengers and I came upon, and drove by, a herd of some 50 or so elk cows and one regal bull elk standing in the midst of his harem with a large and impressive rack of antlers. He clearly had already driven all other male competitors for his women away and was in his element and was most impressive. I admired him. Now, reflecting back on his image, I had a sense that YHWH had orchestrated that encounter with the elk herd particularly for my benefit. He was telling me that I was one of His bull elks and kings. Somehow, all the pain and afflictions of my 66 years of challenged living then seemed well worth such rewards promised to me in the near future.

Over the next several days I felt that YHWH was leading me in several distinct ways. He was revealing to me that He wanted me to reread and update all three of my books, removing my dedications of them to Marsha, and to then write this sequel. Given that I knew then, as I do now, that Yahushua's second coming is imminent, I needed to get my work done swiftly. Today, all three of my prior books have been fully updated and released as new editions. If Yahushua's return occurs before I get this book completed, then so be it: then it was YHWH's will that I not complete it. But unless He pre-empts me, I will continue working to complete this fourth book, which He is now inspiring.

YHWH also inspired me to change my last name to Lionheart, which I have since done, in keeping with the new name YHWH has given to me, as described in Revelation 2:17:

> *"He that hath an ear, let him hear what the Spirit say unto the churches; To him that overcometh will I give to eat of the hidden manna and will give him a white stone,* ***and in the stone a new name written, which no man knoweth saving he that receiveth it.****"* (Bold face for emphasis)

Ordinarily, a man such as myself, who has achieved much, with honesty, integrity, noble character and wisdom brings great honor to his name. However, in my case, eight of the nine demon-possessed psychopaths and tools of the devil who unabashedly sought to destroy me bear the same last name that I was born with. Their collective treachery, betrayals, disrespect and dishonor which they have heaped upon me, a good, godly and righteous man worthy of profound honor and respect, are the most despicable acts any human being could wreak upon another person. And in light of who I am and all I have done that is good, noble and honorable, their treacheries and betrayals toward me are all the more foul, despicable and evil. Since I had no way to compel them to drop my last name, I was left with no alternative but to renounce, disown and disavow any connection I might otherwise have with my prior family members by renouncing, disowning, disavowing and changing my family name forever. One day very soon, YHWH promises me that the family name that I have now renounced and abandoned will be distinctly more foul, disgraceful and shameful than the names of Benedict Arnold and Judas Iscariot for all eternity. It seems to me to be only fitting justice for what those vile creeps and immoral criminals have done to me over many years. Their betrayals, cruelty and heartlessness toward me are inexcusable under any circumstances. In addition, I fully trust YHWH that He will keep His promises and cast all of those wicked fools into eternal torment in the burning lake of fire and brimstone for the evils they are guilty of perpetrating upon me without cause:

> *"Dearly beloved, avenge not yourselves, but rather give place unto wrath: for it is written, Vengeance is mine; I will repay, saith the Lord."* Romans 12:19

I would submit to you that my story of virtually every family member of mine engaging in treachery and betrayal toward me, a supremely good and godly man of impeccable courage and character, is happening now because we are at the bitter end of YHWH's story right before He pulls the plug on the wicked and the foolish of this world gone mad. None of this was the least bit random or accidental. God orchestrated all of it for His good purposes, using me as His empty and fully submitted vessel, to tell His story that, apart from Him, we can do nothing and that with God on our side, who can be against us and prevail? No one can. And that's the ultimate conclusion to God's story of which I am blessed to be used as one of His vessels of honor, through no merit of my own. He did it all.

3. Evidence that the Sixth Seal of Revelation 6 has Now Been Opened

In my first book, *Making Sense Out of a World Gone Mad: A Roadmap for God's Elect Living in the Final Days of the End Times,* at pages 323–327 and in my third book, *Reflections of a Watchman on the Wall in the Final Days of the End Times,* at pages 111–122, I reveal and explain how we can now be quite certain that the prophecies of Revelation 6:12-14 and Matthew 24:29 have now been fulfilled, if we properly understand that most of end times prophecy in the Bible is signified by signs, metaphors, allegories and symbols. That most assuredly is the case with these two particular prophecies, which describe the opening of the sixth seal judgment and its visible effects on earth, which have occurred quite recently, and which signal the imminent second coming of Yahushua, so I am going to take a moment here also to unpack and explain what these two passages are telling us. Let's read the texts together first:

> *"And I beheld when he had opened the sixth seal, and, lo, there was a great earthquake; and the sun became black as sackcloth of hair, and the moon became as blood; And the stars of heaven fell unto the earth, even as a fig tree casteth her untimely figs, when she is shaken of a mighty wind. And the heaven departed as a scroll when it is rolled together; and every mountain and island were moved out of their places."* Revelation 6:12-14

> *"Immediately after the tribulation of those days shall the sun be darkened, and the moon shall not give her light, and the stars shall fall from heaven, and the powers of the heavens shall be shaken:"* Matthew 24:29

I contend that, and I intend to show you why, these two Bible passages are describing one and the same set of consequences on earth from the opening of the sixth seal of Revelation 6:12-14, both of which immediately precede the second coming of Yahushua. Notice that both passages are employing figurative language and metaphors to describe social upheaval and government tyranny, which we are witnessing extensively in our world today. Both passages, using slightly different but very similar words, are describing the sun, moon and stars either growing dark and not giving off their light, or in the case of the stars, they are described as falling to earth, which has much the same effect on the light they give off. Very often, such figurative language is interpreted for us elsewhere in scripture if we know where to look. Having a *New Strong's Exhaustive Concordance of the Bible* available can be very useful in helping us to locate all other Bible passages that employ the same words, in this case, the sun, the moon and stars, to help make sense of the meaning of such figurative language. In the case of these terms, Genesis 37:9-10 explain the meaning of these terms quite clearly:

> *"And he (Joseph, son of Jacob) dreamed yet another dream, and told it his brethren, and said, Behold, I have dreamed a dream more; and, behold, the sun and the moon and the eleven stars made obeisance to me. And he told it to his father, and to his brethren: and his father rebuked him, and said unto him, What is this dream that thou hast dreamed? Shall I and thy mother and thy brethren indeed come to bow down ourselves to thee to the earth?"* (Parenthetical added for clarity)

So Jacob, Joseph's father, upon hearing Joseph's dream, instantly recognized what it was conveying insofar as the sun signified Jacob, his father, the moon symbolized his mother, and the eleven stars were a metaphor for Joseph's eleven brothers in his family. Thus the sun symbolized the major authority in his family, the moon a lesser authority (his mother) and the stars signified even lesser authority in their family. In other contexts, the sun, moon and stars are used to signify governmental authority, as they do in the two passages we are examining together here. So when the metaphorical sun, moon and stars grow dark or fall, such language is symbolizing government oppression and tyranny, such as we are witnessing today, and such as we have been witnessing in America for the last four years, since the fall of 2016 and the Presidential election on November 8, 2016.

Earthquakes are often employed in Bible prophecy to signify social unrest and upheaval. Mountains and islands are often used to symbolize greater and lesser nations, respectively, and when they are described, as they are here, as being moved out of their places, we can be quite certain that all the nations of the world will become deeply troubled.

Any honest observer of our times knows that over the past four years things are not at all right in our world. Just before the prior Presidential election in 2016, WikiLeaks dumped a treasure trove of email correspondence between members of Hillary Clinton's campaign staff and the Democratic National Committee (DNC) that were deeply troubling to many of us, because a number of those emails used coded language commonly used by pedophiles that indicated quite strongly that the leadership of the Clinton campaign, the Clinton Foundation and the Obama administration were engaging in child sex trafficking, child rape, Satanic ritual abuse of children, sacrificing of children and consuming their flesh and blood, that have since become known as the Pizzagate and Pedogate scandals. For the last four years, these horrific stories have been buried, covered up and censored by virtually every mainstream and social media outlet. Nevertheless, many alternative news entities on the internet have gone to great lengths to investigate and expose the rampant abuse of children which America's and the world's rich and powerful routinely engage in to gain demon spirit powers over the rest of us. Those exposed have included top political leaders, Congressmen, Senators, Hollywood and professional sports celebrities, leading businessmen, academics and media personalities.

Donald Trump, from his days as a candidate running for President in 2015 and 2016 up to the present day, has functioned as a wrecking ball of the mainstream media, characterizing most, if not all of them, as fake news. Anyone who still believes that the mainstream media is anything other than a propaganda tool of the global elite conspiracy, the deep state, the swamp, or whatever you choose to call it is strongly delusional and not the least bit sane, interested in the truth or observant.

Mainstream media operations are rapidly losing their audiences and customers to social media and alternative news outlets on the internet and layoffs of reporters and other journalists working for legacy media enterprises are commonplace, as their employers' audiences and advertising revenues shrink dramatically. The mainstream media has effectively made themselves the laughing stock of America with their endless pedaling of lies that the Trump campaign colluded with Russian agents to alter the outcome of the 2016 Presidential election, the fake Christopher Steele dossier, the Mueller Russia investigation that went on for 2 1/2 years and spent over $40 million that came up with nothing, the fake impeachment scam, the Covid fraud, hoax and crime against humanity, and the clearly orchestrated fake riots, looting and violence this past summer which the media characterized as largely peaceful protests (they were not) against systemic racism and police brutality toward blacks in America, that is beyond absurd and totally unsupported by all objective facts.

Most recently, the monstrous voting and election counting fraud of the November 3, 2020 Presidential election is now being revealed and exposed by the alternative media on the internet, Newsmax TV and One America News Network (OAN), while every mainstream media outlet, including the more conservative FOX News, are universally denying these disturbing facts, covering them up and censoring them and falsely claiming that the Trump campaign and his legal teams have failed to provide any real evidence to prove the claims of voter and election fraud. You can only deny obvious criminal acts for a time before you yourself reveal yourself to be a pathological liar, a criminal enterprise and a co-conspirator to the crime yourself, and the mainstream media has now achieved this shameful and disgraceful achievement and well-deserved reputation for it. As such, the mainstream media has deliberately made itself totally irrelevant as a source of real news and a laughing stock deserving of every American's fury, anger and utter disgust. Every last one of them ought to be tarred and feathered and run out of town on a rail in disgrace forever.

Meanwhile, the roles of the CIA, FBI and Department of Justice (DOJ) have rightly been exposed as rogue criminal enterprises which clearly exist to protect the criminal class that runs America from exposure, arrest and prosecution and it has not materially improved during Trump's first four years in office. A case in point is the DOJ's obvious and intentional negligence in the handling of the Jeffrey Epstein sex compromise operation case involving high level elites caught on video having sex with underage minors, on behalf of the Israeli Mossad's blackmail operation of many of America's rich and powerful elites. The same criticism deserves to be leveled at the DOJ for failing to prosecute a number of rogue FBI and DOJ leaders and operatives in connection with their failed attempt to accuse Trump and his 2016 campaign of collusion with the Russians that was alleged to have altered the outcome of the 2016 election, that proved to be totally unfounded and which seriously divided and polarized the American populace over the past four years. While a few high level heads have rolled at the FBI and the DOJ, their entire cultures are ponerized (morally sick) and those two institutions should be shut down and rebuilt from the ground up with entirely new leadership and new staff.

Then we have the discovery by Professor Mark Skidmore and his team of graduate students at Michigan State University in 2016 that $21 trillion dollars has gone missing and is unaccounted for in the financial operations of the Department of Defense (DOD) and of the Department of Housing and Urban Development (HUD). This is on top of the fully acknowledged $25 trillion of ballooning national debt that can only end in the deliberate and intentional devastation and destruction of the value of the U.S. dollar, and a total collapse of the American economy with it. When questioned about this, your government took the fifth and claimed under FASAB (Financial Accounting Standards Advisory Board) Rule 56 that such matters are now a matter of national security (need to be covered up) and therefore cannot be commented on by those responsible for this wanton corruption and evil. It is just one more monstrous government concealment of the truth and cover-up.

Meanwhile, the traditional family in America is effectively dead. Fatherlessness in America that in 1950 stood at 7% is today at over 40% of households with children under the age of 18 living at home. Over 30% of births in America are to unwed mothers. The reported statistics are that 52% of all marriages in America end in divorce. My own observations tell me that the number is actually much higher than this: perhaps as high as 80%. The bedrock protector and provider for all American families, the white Christian man, is today demonized and vilified by a demon-possessed and psychopathic Jewish-controlled legacy media as angry, violent brutes who are deemed guilty of anything they are accused of by rabid, demonized, deceitful, feminist women, until proven otherwise.

America's churches are lifeless too. As I have explained in Chapter 11 of my first book, most churches have sold their souls to the devil by claiming a 501(c)3 tax exempt status that requires them to conceal and eviscerate the truth and replace it with endless lies and distortions. As I have written many times before, all forms of organized religion are, and always have been, demonic and serve the devil, while claiming the precise opposite of this. They are an abomination to YHWH beyond words, and they will pay dearly for their con jobs and their endless frauds very soon.

Our schools and universities are pathetic jokes. Children are taught to disrespect and defy all authority, especially their parents. They are subjected to endless lies, indoctrination and brain washing from the moment they first enter school as kindergartners, and by the time they graduate from high school, most of them are certifiable idiots, morons and fools, unable to think critically for themselves or to restrain themselves from manifesting uncivilized and disrespectful behaviors toward others. Today at universities, students are taught what is politically correct, that is always foolish and evil and not how to think and reason critically for themselves. A college degree today is a waste of time and money and effectively worthless. It wasn't that way nearly 45 years ago when I graduated from college, but things have markedly gone downhill since then.

The most significant global development over the past four years has been the Covid hoax and fraud that has been perpetrated upon the masses of the developed world since mid-March of this year and the reckless and totally unwarranted actions of governmental public health authorities in response to this alleged pandemic by ordering lockdowns, shuttering businesses, mandating the almost universal wearing of face masks in public, social distancing, extensive hand sanitation, the sanitizing of public places and the erection of Plexiglas shields, which in America alone have resulted in 40 to 50 million people becoming unemployed, devastating millions of lives, closing or harming countless businesses and devastating many national economies without reason. Commenting on the reality of our time, here is how Robert F. Kennedy Jr. recently characterized the monstrous corona virus hoax and fraud and its real intent by the global elite conspiracy to enslave humanity in their Orwellian New World Order global surveillance and police state from hell:

> "Every part of our lives will be subject to control. This virus is about training us for submission, training us to do what we're told. To not go to the beach unless we're told, to not kiss our girlfriend without their permission. They're turning us into production units and consuming entities. They are going to rob us not only of our democracy and our liberties, but our souls. They are going to inject us with the medicines they want and they're going to charge us for the diseases they give us. They are going to control every part of our lives. What we are doing

> at Children's Health Defense is using the last instruments of democracy we have left - the Courts - to fight them.
>
> We are in the last battle. We are in the apocalypse. We are fighting for the salvation of humanity. We all knew this was coming, though I never believed it would be in my lifetime. But here it is." [1]

These are sobering words that should stop all of us in our tracks. Paul Craig Roberts, former Assistant Secretary of the U.S. Treasury under President Ronald Reagan, Associate Editor and columnist at the *Wall Street Journal,* a professor of economics at six universities and a social and political commentator who recently penned an article in the *American Free Press* had this to say about what he called The Great Covid Deception of 2020:

> "We have been deceived by public health authorities about Covid-19, partly from public authorities' ignorance of the virus, its spread, and treatment, but mainly on purpose. One reason we were intentionally deceived by public health authorities, and continue to be deceived by them, is to create a market for a Covid vaccination. There are billions of dollars of profits in this, and Big Pharma wants them. The financial connections between public health authorities and Big Pharma means that the World Health Organization, National Institutes of Health, and the Center for Disease Control (CDC) also desire mass vaccinations. If there are not enough people scared out of their wits to voluntarily seek vaccination, the chances are vaccinations will be made mandatory or

---

[1] Michael Henry Dunn. *Robert F. Kennedy, Jr. on the Reality of Our Time.* May 5, 2020, https://www.michaelhenrydunn.com/single-post/2020/05/04/RFK-Jr---We-Are-in-The-Last-Battle?fbclid=IwAR0sIVtdhhVnK3edEBkJb6_X8u0ELA9ywz5MM_P3wnPiidFYLPAzcmSkiys.

your ability to travel, and so forth, will be made dependent on being vaccinated.

Another intentional reason for our deception is the Covid-19 threat justified voting by mail from the safety of one's home. Voting by mail means that no winner can be declared on election night. The mail-in votes will have to be counted as they come in. The delay in declaring an election winner allows time for more propaganda that President Trump has 1) fraudulently rigged his reelection or 2) has lost and won't step down. As the presstitutes speak with one orchestrated voice, whether or not President Trump wins will be buried in reports that he lost and that he refuses to step down or that he won by fraud.

Even if the president survives the color revolution instituted against him, he will be under attack as an illegitimate president just as he was during his first term when he was allegedly elected by "Russian interference." This will suffice to prevent a renewal of his attack on the Globalist Establishment - listen to his first inaugural address - and again sideline his desire to serve peace by reducing the dangerous tensions with Russia, a policy that deprives the military/security complex of its valuable enemy.

As presidents John F. Kennedy and Ronald Reagan learned, reducing tensions with Russia threatens the budget and power of the military/security complex that President Dwight Eisenhower warned Americans against. This complex has more power than the president of the United States. As no one would any longer believe another "lone assassin" explanation, President Trump is being assassinated with false accusations and a color revolution. The president has tried to use Twitter to refute the false accusations, but now the president of the United States is too often censored by Twitter." [2]

Now a group of attorneys, led by consumer protection trial lawyer Reiner Fuellmich of Germany, has announced via a YouTube video (that has since been taken down), that he's one of four German members of a new Corona Investigative Committee, founded on July 10, 2020, that's calling for a massive class action lawsuit against medical, corporate, governmental and media entities for their roles in what the committee describes as an extremely harmful crackdown against human health and civil liberties in response to the fabricated and alleged corona virus pandemic. Fuellmich claims that that the corona virus scandal was "probably the greatest crime against humanity every committed." Crimes against humanity are regulated under Section 7 of the International Criminal Code, according to Fuellmich. [3]

Here is the full transcript of Fuellmich's very informed and disturbing conclusions which he and his other three colleagues of the Corona Investigative Committee have arrived at:

"OPINION

BY REINER FUELLMICH

Originally posted at Global Research

The German Corona Investigative Committee has taken testimony from a large number of international scientists and experts since July 10, 2020.

Their conclusions are the following:

- The corona crisis must be renamed the "Corona Scandal"

---

[2] Paul Craig Roberts, *American Free Press*, Issue 43 & 44, October 19 & 26, pp. 24-25.
[3] Mark Anderson, *American Free Press*, Issue 43 & 44, October 19 & 26, pp. 28-29 and stateofthenation.co/?p=31978.

- It is:
  - The biggest tort case ever
  - The greatest crime against humanity ever committed
- Those responsible must be:
  - **Criminally prosecuted for crimes against humanity**
  - Sued for civil damages
- Deaths
  - There is no excess mortality in any country
  - Corona virus mortality equals seasonal flu
  - 94% of deaths in Bergamo were caused by transferring sick patients to nursing homes where they infected old people with weak immune systems
  - Doctors and hospitals worldwide were paid to declare deceased victims of Covid-19
  - Autopsies showed:
    - Fatalities almost all caused by serious pre-existing conditions
    - Almost all deaths were very old people
    - Sweden (no lockdown) and Britain (strict lockdown) have comparable disease and mortality statistics
  - US states with and without lockdowns have comparable disease and mortality statistics
- Health
  - Hospitals remain empty and some face bankruptcy
  - Populations have T-cell immunity from previous influenza waves
  - Herd immunity needs only 15-25% population infection and is already achieved

    - Only when a person has symptoms can an infection be contagious

- Tests:
    - **Many scientists call this a PCR-test pandemic, not a corona pandemic**
    - **Very healthy and non-infectious people may test positive**
    - **Likelihood of false-positives is 89-94% or near certainty**
    - Prof. Drosten developed his PCR test from an old SARS virus without ever having seen the real Wuhan virus from China
    - The PCR test is not based on scientific facts with respect to infections
    - PCR tests are useless for the detection of infections
    - A positive PCR test does not mean an infection is present or that an intact virus has been found
    - Amplification of samples over 35 cycles is unreliable but WHO recommended 45 cycles
- Illegality:
    - The German government locked down, imposed social-distancing/mask-wearing on the basis of a single opinion
    - The lockdown was imposed when the virus was already retreating
    - The lockdowns were based on non-existent infections
    - Former president of the German federal constitutional court doubted the constitutionality of the corona measures

  - Former UK supreme court judge Lord Sumption concluded there was no factual basis for panic and no legal basis for corona measures
  - German RKI (CDC equivalent) recommended no autopsies be performed
  - Corona measures have no sufficient factual or legal basis, are unconstitutional and must be repealed immediately
  - No serious scientist gives any validity to the infamous Neil Ferguson's false computer models warning of millions of deaths
  - **Mainstream media completely failed to report the true facts of the so-called pandemic**
  - Democracy is in danger of being replaced by fascist totalitarian models
  - Drosten (of PCR test), Tedros of WHO, and others have committed crimes against humanity as defined in the International Criminal Code
  - Politicians can avoid going down with the charlatans and criminals by starting the long overdue public scientific discussion
- Conspiracy:
  - **Politicians and mainstream media deliberately drove populations to panic**
  - Children were calculatedly made to feel responsible "for the painful tortured death of their parents and grandparents if they do not follow Corona rules"
  - The hopeless PCR test is used to create fear and not to diagnose
  - There can be no talk of a second wave
- Injury and damage:

3. Evidence that the Sixth Seal of Revelation 6 has Now Been Opened

- **Evidence of gigantic health and economic damage to populations**
- Anti-corona measures have:
  - Killed innumerable people
  - Destroyed countless companies and individuals worldwide
- Children are being taken away from their parents
- Children are traumatized en masse
- **Bankruptcies are expected in small- and medium-sized businesses**

- Redress:
  - A class action lawsuit must be filed in the USA or Canada, with all affected parties worldwide having the opportunity to join
  - Companies and self-employed people must be compensated for damages

Full Transcript

Hello. I am Reiner Fuellmich and I have been admitted to the Bar in Germany and in California for 26 years. I have been practicing law primarily as a trial lawyer against fraudulent corporations such as Deutsche Bank, formerly one of the world's largest and most respected banks, today one of the most toxic criminal organizations in the world; VW, one of the world's largest and most respected car manufacturers, today notorious for its giant diesel fraud; and Kuehne and Nagel, the world's largest shipping company. We're suing them in a multi-million-dollar bribery case.

I'm also one of four members of the German Corona Investigative Committee. Since July 10, 2020, this Committee has been listening to a large number of international scientists' and experts' testimony to find answers to questions about the corona crisis, which more and more people worldwide are asking. All the above-mentioned cases of corruption and fraud committed by the German corporations pale in comparison in view of the extent of the damage that the corona crisis has caused and continues to cause.

This corona crisis, according to all we know today, must be renamed a "Corona Scandal" and those responsible for it must be criminally prosecuted and sued for civil damages. On a political level, everything must be done to make sure that no one will ever again be in a position of such power as to be able to defraud humanity or to attempt to manipulate us with their corrupt agendas. And for this reason I will now explain to you how and where an international network of lawyers will argue this biggest tort case ever, the corona fraud scandal, which has meanwhile unfolded into probably the greatest crime against humanity ever committed.

Crimes against humanity were first defined in connection with the Nuremberg trials after World War II, that is, when they dealt with the main war criminals of the Third Reich. Crimes against humanity are today regulated in section 7 of the International Criminal Code. The three major questions to be answered in the context of a judicial approach to the corona scandal are:

1. Is there a corona pandemic or is there only a PCR-test pandemic? Specifically, does a positive PCR-test result mean that the person tested is infected with Covid-19, or does it mean absolutely nothing in connection with the Covid-19 infection?

2. Do the so-called anti-corona measures, such as the lockdown, mandatory face masks, social distancing, and quarantine regulations, serve to protect the world's population from corona, or do these measures serve only to make people panic so that they believe – without asking any questions – that their lives are in danger, so that in the end the pharmaceutical and tech industries can generate huge profits from the sale of PCR tests, antigen and antibody tests and vaccines, as well as the harvesting of our genetic fingerprints?

3. Is it true that the German government was massively lobbied, more so than any other country, by the chief protagonists of this so-called corona pandemic, Mr. Drosten, virologist at a charity hospital in Berlin; Mr. Wieler, veterinarian and head of the German equivalent of the CDC, the RKI; and Mr. Tedros, Head of the World Health Organization or WHO; because Germany is known as a particularly disciplined country and was therefore to become a role model for the rest of the world for its strict and, of course, successful adherence to the corona measures?

Answers to these three questions are urgently needed because the allegedly new and highly dangerous coronavirus has not caused any excess mortality anywhere in the world, and certainly not here in Germany. But the anti-corona measures, whose only basis are the PCR-test results, which are in turn all based on the German Drosten test, have, in the meantime, caused the loss of innumerable human lives and have destroyed the economic existence of countless companies and individuals worldwide. In Australia, for example, people are thrown into prison if they do not wear a mask or do not wear it properly, as deemed by the authorities. In the Philippines, people who do not wear a mask or do not wear it properly, in this sense, are getting shot in the head.

Let me first give you a summary of the facts as they present themselves today. The most important thing in a lawsuit is to establish the facts – that is, to find out what actually happened. That is because the application of the law always depends on the facts at issue. If I want to prosecute someone for fraud, I cannot do that by presenting the facts of a car accident. So what happened here regarding the alleged corona pandemic?

The facts laid out below are, to a large extent, the result of the work of the Corona Investigative Committee. This Committee was founded on July 10, 2020 by four lawyers in order to determine, through hearing expert testimony of international scientists and other experts:

1. How dangerous is the virus really?
2. What is the significance of a positive PCR test?
3. What collateral damage has been caused by the corona measures, both with respect to the world population's health, and with respect to the world's economy?

Let me start with a little bit of background information. What happened in May 2019 and then in early 2020? And what happened 12 years earlier with the swine flu, which many of you may have forgotten about? In May 2019, the stronger of the two parties which govern Germany in a grand coalition, the CDU, held a Congress on Global Health, apparently at the instigation of important players from the pharmaceutical industry and the tech industry. At this Congress, the usual suspects, you might say, gave their speeches. Angela Merkel was there, and the German Secretary of Health, Jens Spahn. But, some other people, whom one would not necessarily expect to be present at such a gathering, were also there: Professor Drosten, virologist from the Charite hospital in Berlin; Professor Wieler, veterinarian and Head of the RKI, the German equivalent of the CDC; as well as Mr. Tedros, philosopher and Head of the World Health Organization (WHO). They all gave speeches there. Also present and giving speeches were the chief lobbyists of the world's two largest health funds, namely the Bill and Melinda Gates Foundation and the Wellcome Trust. Less than a year later, these very people called the shots in the proclamation of the worldwide corona pandemic, made sure that mass PCR tests were used to prove mass infections with Covid-19 all over the world, and are now pushing for vaccines to be invented and sold worldwide.

These infections, or rather the positive test results that the PCR tests delivered, in turn became the justification for worldwide lockdowns, social distancing and mandatory face masks. It is important to note at this point that the definition of a pandemic was changed 12 years earlier. Until then, a pandemic was considered to be a disease that spread worldwide and which led to many serious illnesses and deaths.

Suddenly, and for reasons never explained, it was supposed to be a worldwide disease only. Many serious illnesses and many deaths were not required any more to announce a pandemic. Due to this change, the WHO, which is closely intertwined with the global pharmaceutical industry, was able to declare the swine flu pandemic in 2009, with the result that vaccines were produced and sold worldwide on the basis of contracts that have been kept secret until today.

These vaccines proved to be completely unnecessary because the swine flu eventually turned out to be a mild flu, and never became the horrific plague that the pharmaceutical industry and its affiliated universities kept announcing it would turn into, with millions of deaths certain to happen if people didn't get vaccinated. These vaccines also led to serious health problems. About 700 children in Europe fell incurably ill with narcolepsy and are now forever severely disabled. The vaccines bought with millions of taxpayers' money had to be destroyed with even more taxpayers' money. Already then, during the swine flu, the German virologist Drosten was one of those who stirred up panic in the population, repeating over and over again that the swine flu would claim many hundreds of thousands, even millions of deaths all over the world. In the end, it was mainly thanks to Dr. Wolfgang Wodarg and his efforts as a member of the German Bundestag, and also a member of the Council of Europe, that this hoax was brought to an end before it would lead to even more serious consequences.

Fast forward to March of 2020, when the German Bundestag announced an Epidemic Situation of National Importance, which is the German equivalent of a pandemic in March of 2020 and, based on this, the lockdown with the suspension of all essential constitutional rights for an unforeseeable time, there was only one single opinion on which the Federal Government in Germany based its decision. In an outrageous violation of the universally accepted principle "audiatur et altera pars", which means that one must also hear the other side, the only person they listened to was Mr. Drosten.

That is the very person whose horrific, panic-inducing prognoses had proved to be catastrophically false 12 years earlier. We know this because a whistleblower named David Sieber, a member of the Green Party, told us about it. He did so first on August 29, 2020 in Berlin, in the context of an event at which Robert F. Kennedy, Jr. also took part, and at which both men gave speeches. And he did so afterwards in one of the sessions of our Corona Committee.

The reason he did this is that he had become increasingly skeptical about the official narrative propagated by politicians and the mainstream media. He had therefore undertaken an effort to find out about other scientists' opinions and had found them on the Internet. There, he realized that there were a number of highly renowned scientists who held a completely different opinion, which contradicted the horrific prognoses of Mr. Drosten. They assumed – and still do assume – that there was no disease that went beyond the gravity of the seasonal flu, that the population had already acquired cross- or T-cell immunity against this allegedly new virus, and that there was therefore no reason for any special measures, and certainly not for vaccinations.

These scientists include **Professor John Ioannidis** of Stanford University in California, a specialist in statistics and epidemiology, as well as public health, and at the same time the most quoted scientist in the world; **Professor Michael Levitt**, Nobel prize-winner for chemistry and also a biophysicist at Stanford University; the German professors **Kary Mölling, Sucharit Bhakti, Klud Wittkowski**, as well as **Stefan Homburg**; and now many, many more scientists and doctors worldwide, including Dr. Mike Yeadon. Dr. Mike Yeadon is the former Vice-President and Scientific Director of Pfizer, one of the largest pharmaceutical companies in the world. I will talk some more about him a little later.

At the end of March, beginning of April of 2020, Mr. Sieber turned to the leadership of his Green Party with the knowledge he had accumulated, and suggested that they present these other scientific opinions to the public and explain that, contrary to Mr. Drosten's doomsday prophecies, there was no reason for the public to panic. Incidentally, Lord Sumption, who served as a judge at the British Supreme Court from 2012 to 2018, had done the very same thing at the very same time and had come to the very same conclusion: that there was no factual basis for panic and no legal basis for the corona measures. Likewise, the former President of the German federal constitutional court expressed – albeit more cautiously – serious doubts that the corona measures were constitutional. But instead of taking note of these other opinions and discussing them with David Sieber, the Green Party leadership declared that Mr. Drosten's panic messages were good enough for the Green Party. Remember, they're not a member of the ruling coalition; they're the opposition. Still, that was enough for them, just as it had been good enough for the Federal Government as a basis for its lockdown decision, they said. They subsequently, the Green Party leadership, called David Sieber a conspiracy theorist, without ever having considered the content of his information, and then stripped him of his mandates.

Now let's take a look at the current actual situation regarding the virus's danger, the complete uselessness of PCR tests for the detection of infections, and the lockdowns based on non-existent infections. In the meantime, we know that the health care systems were never in danger of becoming overwhelmed by Covid-19. On the contrary, many hospitals remain empty to this day and some are now facing bankruptcy. The hospital ship Comfort, which anchored in New York at the time, and could have accommodated a thousand patients, never accommodated more than some 20 patients. Nowhere was there any excess mortality. Studies carried out by Professor Ioannidis and others have shown that the mortality of corona is equivalent to that of the seasonal flu. Even the pictures from Bergamo and New York that were used to demonstrate to the world that panic was in order proved to be deliberately misleading.

Then, the so-called "Panic Paper" was leaked, which was written by the German Department of the Interior. Its classified content shows beyond a shadow of a doubt that, in fact, the population was deliberately driven to panic by politicians and mainstream media. The accompanying irresponsible statements of the Head of the RKI – remember the [German] CDC – Mr. Wieler, who repeatedly and excitedly announced that the corona measures must be followed unconditionally by the population without them asking any question, shows that that he followed the script verbatim. In his public statements, he kept announcing that the situation was very grave and threatening, although the figures compiled by his own Institute proved the exact opposite.

Among other things, the "Panic Paper" calls for children to be made to feel responsible – and I quote – "for the painful tortured death of their parents and grandparents if they do not follow the corona rules", that is, if they do not wash their hands constantly and don't stay away from their grandparents. A word of clarification: in Bergamo, the vast majority of deaths, 94% to be exact, turned out to be the result not of Covid-19, but rather the consequence of the government deciding to transfer sick patients, sick with probably the cold or seasonal flu, from hospitals to nursing homes in order to make room at the hospitals for all the Covid patients, who ultimately never arrived. There, at the nursing homes, they then infected old people with a severely weakened immune system, usually as a result of pre-existing medical conditions. In addition, a flu vaccination, which had previously been administered, had further weakened the immune systems of the people in the nursing homes. In New York, only some, but by far not all hospitals were overwhelmed. Many people, most of whom were again elderly and had serious pre-existing medical conditions, and most of whom, had it not been for the panic-mongering, would have just stayed at home to recover, raced to the hospitals. There, many of them fell victim to healthcare-associated infections (or nosocomial infections) on the one hand, and incidents of malpractice on the other hand, for example, by being put on a respirator rather than receiving oxygen through an oxygen mask. Again, to clarify: Covid-19, this is the current state of affairs, is a dangerous disease, just like the seasonal flu is a dangerous disease. And of course,

Covid-19, just like the seasonal flu, may sometimes take a severe clinical course and will sometimes kill patients.

However, as autopsies have shown, which were carried out in Germany in particular, by the forensic scientist Professor Klaus Püschel in Hamburg, the fatalities he examined had almost all been caused by serious pre-existing conditions, and almost all of the people who had died, died at a very old age, just like in Italy, meaning they had lived beyond their average life expectancy.

In this context, the following should also be mentioned: the German RKI – that is, again the equivalent of the CDC – had initially, strangely enough, recommended that no autopsies be performed. And there are numerous credible reports that doctors and hospitals worldwide had been paid money for declaring a deceased person a victim of Covid-19 rather than writing down the true cause of death on the death certificate, for example a heart attack or a gunshot wound. Without the autopsies, we would never know that the overwhelming majority of the alleged Covid-19 victims had died of completely different diseases, but not of Covid-19. The assertion that the lockdown was necessary because there were so many different infections with SARS-COV-2, and because the healthcare systems would be overwhelmed is wrong for three reasons, as we have learned from the hearings we conducted with the Corona Committee, and from other data that has become available in the meantime:

A. The lockdown was imposed when the virus was already retreating. By the time the lockdown was imposed, the alleged infection rates were already dropping again.

B. There's already protection from the virus because of cross- or T-cell immunity. Apart from the above mentioned lockdown being imposed when the infection rates were already dropping, there is also cross- or T-cell immunity in the general population against the corona viruses contained in every flu or influenza wave. This is true, even if this time around, a slightly different strain of the coronavirus was at work. And that is because the body's own immune system remembers every virus it has ever battled in the past, and from this experience, it also recognizes a supposedly new, but still similar, strain of the virus from the corona family. Incidentally, that's how the PCR test for the detection of an infection was invented by now infamous Professor Drosten.

At the beginning of January of 2020, based on this very basic knowledge, Mr. Drosten developed his PCR test, which supposedly detects an infection with SARS-COV-2, without ever having seen the real Wuhan virus from China, only having learned from social media reports that there was something going on in Wuhan, he started tinkering on his computer with what would become his corona PCR test. For this, he used an old SARS virus, hoping it would be sufficiently similar to the allegedly new strain of the coronavirus found in Wuhan. Then, he sent the result of his computer tinkering to China to determine whether the victims of the alleged new coronavirus tested positive. They did.

And that was enough for the World Health Organization to sound the pandemic alarm and to recommend the worldwide use of the Drosten PCR test for the detection of infections with the virus now called SARS-COV-2. Drosten's opinion and advice was – this must be emphasized once again – the only source for the German government when it announced the lockdown as well as the rules for social distancing and the mandatory wearing of masks. And – this must also be emphasized once again – Germany apparently became the center of especially massive lobbying by the pharmaceutical and tech industry because the world, with reference to the allegedly disciplined Germans, should do as the Germans do in order to survive the pandemic.

C. And this is the most important part of our fact-finding: **the PCR test is being used on the basis of false statements, NOT based on scientific facts with respect to infections.** In the meantime, we have learned that these PCR tests, contrary to the assertions of Messrs. Drosten, Wieler and the WHO, do NOT give any indication of an infection with any virus, let alone an infection with SARS-COV-2. Not only are

PCR tests expressly not approved for diagnostic purposes, as is correctly noted on leaflets coming with these tests, and as the inventor of the PCR test, Kary Mullis, has repeatedly emphasized. Instead, they're simply incapable of diagnosing any disease. That is: contrary to the assertions of Drosten, Wieler and the WHO, which they have been making since the proclamation of the pandemic, a positive PCR-test result does not mean that an infection is present. If someone tests positive, it does NOT mean that they're infected with anything, let alone with the contagious SARS-COV-2 virus.

Even the United States CDC, even this institution agrees with this, and I quote directly from page 38 of one of its publications on the coronavirus and the PCR tests, dated July 13, 2020. First bullet point says:

"Detection of viral RNA may not indicate the presence of infectious virus or that 2019 nCOV [novel coronavirus] is the causative agent for clinical symptoms."

Second bullet point says:

"The performance of this test has not been established for monitoring treatment of 2019 nCOV infection."

Third bullet point says:

"This test cannot rule out diseases caused by other bacterial or viral pathogens."

It is still not clear whether there has ever been a scientifically correct isolation of the Wuhan virus, so that nobody knows exactly what we're looking for when we test, especially since this virus, just like the flu viruses, mutates quickly. **The PCR swabs take one or two sequences of a molecule that are invisible to the human eye and therefore need to be amplified in many cycles to make it visible**. Everything over 35 cycles is – as reported by the New York Times and others – considered completely unreliable and scientifically unjustifiable. However, **the Drosten test, as well as the WHO-recommended tests that followed his example, are set to 45 cycles**. Can that be because of the desire to produce as many positive results as possible and thereby provide the basis for the false assumption that a large number of infections have been detected?

The test cannot distinguish inactive and reproductive matter. **That means that a positive result may happen because the test detects, for example, a piece of debris, a fragment of a molecule, which may signal nothing else than that the immune system of the person tested won a battle with a common cold in the past**. Even Drosten himself declared in an interview with a German business magazine in 2014, at that time concerning the alleged detection of an infection with the MERS virus, allegedly with the help of the PCR test, that these PCR tests are so highly sensitive that even very healthy and non-infectious people may test positive. At that time, he also became very much aware of the powerful role of a panic and fear-mongering media, as you'll see at the end of the following quote. He said then, in this interview: "If, for example, such a pathogen scurries over the nasal mucosa of a nurse for a day or so without her getting sick or noticing anything, then she's suddenly a MERS case. This could also explain the explosion of case numbers in Saudi Arabia. In addition, the media there have made this into an incredible sensation."

Has he forgotten this? Or is he deliberately concealing this in the corona context because corona is a very lucrative business opportunity for the pharmaceutical industry as a whole? And for Mr. Alford Lund, his co-author in many studies and also a PCR-test producer. In my view, it is completely implausible that he forgot in 2020 what he knew about the PCR tests and told the business magazine in 2014.

In short, this test cannot detect any infection, contrary to all false claims stating that it can. An infection, a so-called "hot" infection, requires that the virus, or rather a fragment of a molecule which may be a virus, is not just found somewhere, for example, in the throat of a person without causing any damage – that would be a "cold" infection. Rather, a "hot" infection requires that the virus penetrates into the cells, replicates there and causes symptoms such as headaches or a sore throat. Only then is a person really infected in the sense of a "hot" infection, because only then is a person contagious, that is, able to infect others. Until then, it is completely harmless for both the host and all other people that the host comes into contact with.

Once again, this means that positive test results, contrary to all other claims by Drosten, Wieler, or the WHO, mean nothing with respect to infections, as even the CDC knows, as quoted above.

Meanwhile, a number of highly respected scientists worldwide assume that there has never been a corona pandemic, but only **a PCR-test pandemic**. This is the conclusion reached by many German scientists, such as professors Bhakti, Reiss, Mölling, Hockertz, Walach and many others, including the above-mentioned Professor John Ioannidis, and the Nobel laureate, Professor Michael Levitt from Stanford University.

The most recent such opinion is that of the aforementioned **Dr. Mike Yeadon**, a former Vice-President and Chief Science Officer at Pfizer, who held this position for 16 years. He and his co-authors, all well-known scientists, published a scientific paper in September of 2020 and he wrote a corresponding magazine article on September 20, 2020. Among other things, he and they state – and I quote:

"We're basing our government policy, our economic policy, and the policy of restricting fundamental rights, presumably on completely wrong data and assumptions about the coronavirus. If it weren't for the test results that are constantly reported in the media, the pandemic would be over because nothing really happened. Of course, there are some serious individual cases of illness, but there are also some in every flu epidemic. There was a real wave of disease in March and April, but since then, everything has gone back to normal. Only the positive results rise and sink wildly again and again, depending on how many tests are carried out. But the real cases of illnesses are over. There can be no talk of a second wave. The allegedly new strain of the coronavirus is …"

– Dr. Yeadon continues –

"... only new in that it is a new type of the long-known corona virus. There are at least four coronaviruses that are endemic and cause some of the common colds we experience, especially in winter. They all have a striking sequence similarity to the coronavirus, and because the human immune system recognizes the similarity to the virus that has now allegedly been newly discovered, a T-cell immunity has long existed in this respect. 30 per cent of the population had this before the allegedly new virus even appeared. Therefore, it is sufficient for the so-called herd immunity that 15 to 25 per cent of the population are infected with the allegedly new coronavirus to stop the further spread of the virus. And this has long been the case."

Regarding the all-important PCR tests, Yeadon writes, in a piece called "Lies, Damned Lies and Health Statistics: The Deadly Danger of False Positives," dated September 20, 2020, and I quote:

"The likelihood of an apparently positive case being a false positive is between 89 to 94 per cent, or near certainty."

Dr. Yeadon, in agreement with the professors of immunology Kamera from Germany, Kappel from the Netherlands, and Cahill from Ireland, as well as the microbiologist Dr. Arve from Austria, all of whom testified before the German Corona Committee, explicitly points out that a positive test does not mean that an intact virus has been found.

The authors explain that what the PCR test actually measures is – and I quote:

"Simply the presence of partial RNA sequences present in the intact virus, which could be a piece of dead virus, which cannot make the subject sick, and cannot be transmitted, and cannot make anyone else sick."

Because of the complete unsuitability of the test for the detection of infectious diseases – tested positive in goats, sheep, papayas and even chicken wings – Oxford Professor Carl Heneghan, Director of the Centre for Evidence-Based Medicine, writes that the Covid virus would never disappear if this test practice were to be continued, but would always be falsely detected in much of what is tested. Lockdowns, as Yeadon and his colleagues found out, do not work. Sweden, with its laissez-faire approach, and Great Britain, with its strict lockdown, for example, have completely comparable disease and mortality statistics. The same was found by US scientists concerning the different US states. It makes no difference to the incidence of disease whether a state implements a lockdown or not.

With regard to the now infamous Imperial College of London's Professor Neil Ferguson and his completely false computer models warning of millions of deaths, he says that – and I quote: "No serious scientist gives any validity to Ferguson's model." He points out with thinly veiled contempt – again I quote:

"It's important that you know, most scientists don't accept that it …" – that is, Ferguson's model – "was even faintly right. But the government is still wedded to the model." Ferguson predicted 40 thousand corona deaths in Sweden by May and 100 thousand by June, but it remained at 5,800 which, according to the Swedish authorities, is equivalent to a mild flu. If the PCR tests had not been used as a diagnostic tool for corona infections, there would not be a pandemic and there would be no lockdowns, but everything would have been perceived as just a medium or light wave of influenza, these scientists conclude. Dr. Yeadon in his piece, "Lies, Damned Lies and Health Statistics: The Deadly Danger of False Positives, writes: "This test is fatally flawed and must immediately be withdrawn and never used again in this setting, unless shown to be fixed." And, towards the end of that article, "I have explained how a hopelessly performing diagnostic test has been, and continues to be used, not for diagnosis of disease, but it seems solely to create fear".

Now let's take a look at the current actual situation regarding the severe damage caused by the lockdowns and other measures. Another detailed paper, written by a German official in the Department of the Interior, who is responsible for risk assessment and the protection of the population against risks, was leaked recently. It is now called the "False Alarm" paper. This paper comes to the conclusion that there was and is no sufficient evidence for serious health risks for the population as claimed by Drosten, Wieler and the WHO, but – the author says – there's very much evidence of the corona measures causing gigantic health and economic damage to the population, which he then describes in detail in this paper. This, he concludes, will lead to very high claims for damages, which the government will be held responsible for. This has now become reality, but the paper's author was suspended.

More and more scientists, but also lawyers, recognize that, as a result of the deliberate panic-mongering, and the corona measures enabled by this panic, democracy is in great danger of being replaced by fascist totalitarian models. As I already mentioned above, in Australia, people who do not wear the masks, which more and more studies show are hazardous to health, or who allegedly do not wear them correctly, are arrested, handcuffed and thrown into jail. In the Philippines, they run the risk of getting shot, but even in Germany and in other previously civilized countries, children are taken away from their parents if they do not comply with quarantine regulations, distance regulations, and mask-wearing regulations. According to psychologists and psychotherapists who testified before the Corona Committee, children are traumatized en masse, with the worst psychological consequences yet to be expected in the medium- and long-term. In Germany alone, bankruptcies are expected in the fall to strike small- and medium-sized businesses, which form the backbone of the economy. This will result in incalculable tax losses and incalculably high and long-term social security money transfers for – among other things – unemployment benefits.

Since, in the meantime, pretty much everybody is beginning to understand the full devastating impact of the completely unfounded corona measures, I will refrain from detailing this any further.

3. Evidence that the Sixth Seal of Revelation 6 has Now Been Opened

Let me now give you a summary of the legal consequences. The most difficult part of a lawyer's work is always to establish the true facts, not the application of the legal rules to these facts. Unfortunately, a German lawyer does not learn this at law school but his Anglo-American counterparts do get the necessary training for this at their law schools. And probably for this reason, but also because of the much more pronounced independence of the Anglo-American judiciary, the Anglo-American law of evidence is much more effective in practice than the German one. A court of law can only decide a legal dispute correctly if it has previously determined the facts correctly, which is not possible without looking at all the evidence. And that's why the law of evidence is so important. On the basis of the facts summarized above, in particular those established with the help of the work of the German Corona Committee, the legal evaluation is actually simple. It is simple for all civilized legal systems, regardless of whether these legal systems are based on civil law, which follows the Roman law more closely, or whether they are based on Anglo-American common law, which is only loosely connected to Roman law.

Let's first take a look at the unconstitutionality of the measures. A number of German law professors, including professors Kingreen, Morswig, Jungbluth and Vosgerau have stated, either in written expert opinions or in interviews, in line with the serious doubts expressed by the former president of the federal constitutional court with respect to the constitutionality of the corona measures, that these measures – the corona measures – are without a sufficient factual basis, and also without a sufficient legal basis, and are therefore unconstitutional and must be repealed immediately. Very recently, a judge, Thorsten Schleif is his name, declared publicly that the German judiciary, just like the general public, has been so panic-stricken that it was no longer able to administer justice properly. He says that the courts of law – and I quote – "have all too quickly waved through coercive measures which, for millions of people all over Germany, represent massive suspensions of their constitutional rights. He points out that German citizens – again I quote – "are currently experiencing the most serious encroachment on their constitutional rights since the founding of the federal republic of Germany in 1949". In order to contain the corona pandemic, federal and state governments have intervened, he says, massively, and in part threatening the very existence of the country as it is guaranteed by the constitutional rights of the people.

What about fraud, intentional infliction of damage and crimes against humanity?

Based on the rules of criminal law, **asserting false facts concerning the PCR tests or intentional misrepresentation**, as it was committed by Messrs. Drosten, Wieler and Tedros, as well as the WHO, can only be assessed as fraud. Based on the rules of civil tort law, this translates into intentional infliction of damage. The German professor of civil law, Martin Schwab, supports this finding in public interviews. In a comprehensive legal opinion of around 180 pages, he has familiarized himself with the subject matter like no other legal scholar has done thus far and, in particular, has provided a detailed account of the complete failure of the mainstream media to report on the true facts of this so-called pandemic. Messrs. Drosten, Wieler and Tedros of the WHO all knew, based on their own expertise or the expertise of their institutions, that the PCR tests cannot provide any information about infections, but asserted over and over again to the general public that they can, with their counterparts all over the world repeating this. And they all knew and accepted that, on the basis of their recommendations, the governments of the world would decide on lockdowns, the rules for social distancing, and mandatory wearing of masks, the latter representing a very serious health hazard, as more and more independent studies and expert statements show. Under the rules of civil tort law, all those who have been harmed by these PCR-test-induced lockdowns are entitled to receive full compensation for their losses. In particular, there is a duty to compensate – that is, a duty to pay damages for the loss of profits suffered by companies and self-employed employed persons as a result of the lockdown and other measures.

3. Evidence that the Sixth Seal of Revelation 6 has Now Been Opened

In the meantime, however, the anti-corona measures have caused, and continue to cause, such devastating damage to the world population's health and economy that the crimes committed by Messrs. Drosten, Wieler and the WHO must be legally qualified as actual crimes against humanity, as defined in section 7 of the International Criminal Code.

How can we do something? What can we do? Well, the class action is the best route to compensatory damages and to political consequences. The so-called class action lawsuit is based on English law and exists today in the USA and in Canada. It enables a court of law to allow a complaint for damages to be tried as a class action lawsuit at the request of a plaintiff if:

1. As a result of a damage-inducing event …
2. A large number of people suffer the same type of damage.

Phrased differently, a judge can allow a class-action lawsuit to go forward if common questions of law and fact make up the vital component of the lawsuit. Here, the common questions of law and fact revolve around the worldwide PCR-test-based lockdowns and its consequences. Just like the VW diesel passenger cars were functioning products, but they were defective due to a so-called defeat device because they didn't comply with the emissions standards, so too the PCR tests – which are perfectly good products in other settings – are defective products when it comes to the diagnosis of infections. Now, if an American or Canadian company or an American or Canadian individual decides to sue these persons in the United States or Canada for damages, then the court called upon to resolve this dispute may, upon request, allow this complaint to be tried as a class action lawsuit.

If this happens, all affected parties worldwide will be informed about this through publications in the mainstream media and will thus have the opportunity to join this class action within a certain period of time, to be determined by the court. It should be emphasized that nobody must join the class action, but every injured party can join the class.

The advantage of the class action is that only one trial is needed, namely to try the complaint of a representative plaintiff who is affected in a manner typical of everyone else in the class. This is, firstly, cheaper, and secondly, faster than hundreds of thousands or more individual lawsuits. And thirdly, it imposes less of a burden on the courts. Fourthly, as a rule it allows a much more precise examination of the accusations than would be possible in the context of hundreds of thousands, or more likely in this corona setting, even millions of individual lawsuits.

In particular, the well-established and proven Anglo-American law of evidence, with its pre-trial discovery, is applicable. This requires that all evidence relevant for the determination of the lawsuit be put on the table. In contrast to the typical situation in German lawsuits with structural imbalance, that is, lawsuits involving on the one hand a consumer, and on the other hand a powerful corporation, the withholding or even destruction of evidence is not without consequence; rather the party withholding or even destroying evidence loses the case under these evidence rules.

Here in Germany, a group of tort lawyers have banded together to help their clients with recovery of damages. They have provided all relevant information and forms for German plaintiffs to both estimate how much damage they have suffered and join the group or class of plaintiffs who will later join the class action when it goes forward either in Canada or the US. Initially, this group of lawyers had considered to also collect and manage the claims for damages of other, non-German plaintiffs, but this proved to be unmanageable.

However, through an international lawyers' network, which is growing larger by the day, the German group of attorneys provides to all of their colleagues in all other countries, free of charge, all relevant information, including expert opinions and testimonies of experts showing that the PCR tests cannot detect infections. And they also provide them with all relevant information as to how they can prepare and bundle the claims for damages of their clients so that, they too, can assert their clients' claims for damages, either in their home country's courts of law, or within the framework of the class action, as explained above.

These scandalous corona facts, gathered mostly by the Corona Committee and summarized above, are the very same facts that will soon be proven to be true either in one court of law, or in many courts of law all over the world.

These are the facts that will pull the masks off the faces of all those responsible for these crimes. To the politicians who believe those corrupt people, these facts are hereby offered as a lifeline that can help you readjust your course of action, and start the long overdue public scientific discussion, and not go down with those charlatans and criminals.

Thank you." [4]

Many accomplished medical researchers and physicians have come out publicly, strongly opposing the claims of governmental public health authorities concerning the dangers of the corona virus and arguing strenuously against the tyrannical and senseless measures which the governments of the developed world have imposed on their populations to their grave physical, financial and emotional harm. These credible health experts have been universally censored, blocked and shut down from communicating their important findings and conclusions to the general public in a campaign of censorship and truth suppression that can only be described as Orwellian dystopia. The world, and its devil-worshipping puppets posing as our leaders, have literally gone insane! And almost no one dares to say a peep, out of fear and cowardice as to what others may adversely think about them. This is the inevitable end point of a society and a civilization that has been thoroughly demonized and brainwashed into tolerating and going along to get along with that which is pure evil.

Dr. Judy A. Mikovits and Kent Heckenlively, JD have published two books this year, one entitled, *The Case Against*

---

[4] https://www.globalresearch.ca/video-crimes-against-humanity-the-german-corona-investigation/5725795

Masks: Ten Reasons Why Mask Use Should be Limited, and the other one entitled, *Plague of Corruption: Restoring Faith in the Promise of Science*, both of which ought to be required reading for anyone trying to make coherent sense out of the Covid fraud and hoax. These books have also been actively suppressed, silenced and censored by the legacy and social media thought police in order to continue to advance the agenda of the New World Order thugs behind this hoax and fraud. The aim of The Powers That Be (TPTB) here is very simple:

> "Deviant behavior, left unchallenged, becomes the accepted norm." — Aldo Leopold

Therefore, the globalist, Talmudic Jewish, synagogue of Satan is doing everything in its power to silence the truth and truth tellers who are challenging their lies, any way they can, so that their lies and deviant behaviors can defile humanity unopposed and unchallenged. This is the principle behind the rampant censorship many of us whistleblowers and truth tellers have encountered on Facebook, Twitter, YouTube and other social media platforms and none of them are exempt, because they all are in on this and part of the globalist cabal, the first beast political and economic system described in Revelation 13. I personally have been banned from posting on Facebook 23 times for a total of 617 days to date since early 2016 for posting comments that reveal and expose exactly who the Talmudic Jews really are and for exposing their many hideous lies and crimes against humanity throughout the last 2,000 years of world history. More recently, YouTube has removed my account for my many replies to YouTube videos which allegedly violate their community standards. That's just double-speak for censorship and silencing the inconvenient truths I teach. Has it deterred me? Not one bit. They are just two more teaching tools and platforms for me to reach audiences I might not otherwise be able to access with the many truths I teach. I am knowingly using the tools of the devil against him and his followers in a way that I know torments the daylights out of them. That alone gives me great pleasure and delight.

3. Evidence that the Sixth Seal of Revelation 6 has Now Been Opened

When any honest and well-informed researcher examines the claims of the world health authorities concerning the Covid hoax and fraud, one cannot help but arrive at the following simple and obvious conclusions:

1. The World Health Organization (WHO) and Center for Disease Control (CDC) referring to the Covid scam as a pandemic (as opposed to an outbreak of some form of pathogen) was only possible by committing fraud with the word pandemic, as Reiner Fuellmich reported above, in which sometime in 2007, the definition of pandemic was altered. As Fuellmich states, "Until then, a pandemic was considered to be a disease that spread worldwide and which led to many serious illnesses and deaths. Suddenly, and for reasons never explained, it was supposed to be a worldwide disease only. Many serious illnesses and many deaths were not required any more to announce a pandemic."
2. The mortality rate of the Covid disease or likely bio-weapon is relatively benign, according to CDC reported statistics. Overall, the survival rate I have seen reported stands at roughly 99.76%, or a mortality rate which is the inverse of this at 0.24% of those reported as infected with the alleged virus, as measured by the PCR test which Fuellmich reports as generating 86-94% false positives! Furthermore, the reported deaths attributed to Covid had an average of 2.6 co-morbidities, meaning other life-threatening conditions and the vast majority of reported deaths occurred among the elderly and the infirm with no idea as to real causality. So what can we conclude regarding the lethality of this alleged virus? Frankly speaking, Covid is no more lethal than the annual flu, for which the government and public health authority mandates to curtail the spread of this pathogen are beyond absurd and totally unwarranted and unjustified and there is nothing the least bit scientific about the Covid directives. Combined, the fear mongering concerning

the dangers of Covid and the governmental mandates in response to it amount to the most elaborate form of psychological warfare ever perpetrated upon the global population of humanity.

3. As I understand it, the Covid virus has yet to be isolated in any medical research lab. Instead, a PCR test that its developer has clearly indicated is wholly inadequate for diagnosing any disease is being used as a proxy for an as-yet-unproven pathogen. As a result of the extraordinarily high rate of false positives generated by this meaningless test, the number of reported new Covid cases is equally unreliable and lacking in scientific or medical credibility. Thus, any public health response to this alleged pathogen is clearly manipulated and contrived to generate a political, social and economic global disaster through the endless repetition of lies propagated by the mendacious, propaganda-spewing mainstream media. Anyone in any position of authority who promotes the government Covid mandates is a pathological liar who should be fired immediately, tarred and feathered, and run out of town on a rail. Furthermore, they should be shamed and disgraced for all eternity.

4. It could not be more obvious that TPTB, who comprise the global elite conspiracy of Satan worshippers, many of whom are clearly psychopaths and pathological liars, is to psychologically terrorize the populations of nations in the developed world, in order to reset the global paradigm into one in which the masses simply give up and obey whatever directives their psychopath globalist masters order them to do that usually will have no basis in fact or sound logical reasoning, and which often are designed to harm them, as is most certainly the case with respect to mandates to wear face masks that do not provide any real protection to the wearers or the public they encounter.

5. What is most telling and disturbing of all is that these conclusions do not require any great scientific

> knowledge or logical reasoning skills to arrive at. They are painfully obvious. And yet, well over 95% of the population in America has succumbed to this psychological terror campaign without so much as a peep of objection. Fearfulness explains their behavior: either fear of what others might think of them for not wearing a mask in public, or in a lesser number of cases, unwarranted fear concerning the dangers of the Covid pathogen to their own health. This should alarm many people, inasmuch as Revelation 21:8 reveals that all those who are fearful *"shall have their part in the lake which burneth with fire and brimstone."* This warning pertains to virtually everyone alive today who is routinely complying with mandates to wear masks and otherwise validate and legitimize this profound fraud.

The significance of the Covid hoax and fraud cannot be overstated. This event and public health authorities' response to it has forced the global elite conspiracy to emerge out into the open for all the public to see and to see their full agenda. The founder of the World Economic Forum, Klaus Schwab, has co-authored and published a book this year entitled, *COVID-19: The Great Reset*, which is making the case that the global plandemic, or scamdemic, if you please, providentially provides the crisis conditions needed to transform the world to reflect the vision the Illuminati and their ilk have to usher in their New World Order from hell, with a one world government, a new one world (digital) currency, and a one world religion, which secretly worships Lucifer, aka Satan, aka the devil, the god of this world, the father of lies and the destroyer. By now, most of humanity is so brainwashed and strongly deluded (see 2 Thessalonians 2:10-12) that they are not even going to bat an eye at what these events are telling a few of us. The simple fact is that the Covid crisis is ripping our world and nation apart, and causing well over 90% of the populace to be fearful for their health, when the objective facts reveal that such fear is totally unwarranted for the vast majority of us. We are being psychologically terrorized with malicious lies and fraud that appears unstoppable; unless YHWH intervenes, which all the signs seem to be pointing to quite clearly, for those with the ears to hear and the eyes to see these sorts of things.

To put these revelations into their full and proper context and perspective, Vatican whistleblower, Archbishop Carlo Maria Viganò, addressed this open letter to President Trump just days before the November 3, 2020 Presidential election that exposes the full extent of the Covid scam and its ultimate aims:

"OPEN LETTER
TO THE PRESIDENT OF THE UNITED STATES OF AMERICA
DONALD J. TRUMP

Sunday, October 25, 2020
Solemnity of Christ the King

Mister President,

Allow me to address you at this hour in which the fate of the whole world is being threatened by a global conspiracy against God and humanity. I write to you as an Archbishop, as a Successor of the Apostles, as the former Apostolic Nuncio to the United States of America. I am writing to you in the midst of the silence of both civil and religious authorities. May you accept these words of mine as the "voice of one crying out in the desert." (Jn 1:23)

As I said when I wrote my letter to you in June, this historical moment sees the forces of Evil aligned in a battle without quarter against the forces of Good; forces of Evil that appear powerful and organized as they oppose the children of Light, who are disoriented, and disorganized, abandoned by their temporal and spiritual leaders.

Daily we sense the attacks multiplying of those who want to destroy the very basis of society: the natural family, respect for human life, love of country, freedom of education and business. We see heads of nations and religious leaders pandering to this suicide of Western culture and its Christian soul, while the fundamental rights of citizens and believers are denied in the name of a health emergency that it revealing itself more and more fully as instrumental to the establishment of an inhuman faceless tyranny.

A global plan called the ***Great Reset*** is underway. Its architect is a global élite that wants to subdue all of humanity, imposing coercive measures with which to drastically limit individual freedoms and those of entire populations. In several nations this plan has already been approved and financed; in others it is still in an early stage. Behind the world leaders who are accomplices and executors of this infernal project, there are unscrupulous characters who finance the *World Economic Forum* and *Event 201*, promoting their agenda.

The purpose of the *Great Reset* is the imposition of a health dictatorship aiming at the imposition of liberticidal measures, hidden behind tempting promises of ensuring a universal income and cancelling individual debt. The price of these concessions from the International Monetary Fund will be the renunciation of private property and adherence to a program of vaccination against Covid-19 and Covid-21 promoted by Bill Gates with the collaboration of the main pharmaceutical groups. Beyond the enormous economic interests that motivate the promoters of the *Great Reset*, the imposition of the vaccination will be accompanied by the requirement of a health passport and a digital ID, with the consequent contact tracing of the population of the entire world. Those who do not accept these measures will be confined to detention camps or placed under house arrest, and all their assets will be confiscated.

Mr. President, I imagine that you are already aware that in some countries the *Great Reset* will be activated between the end of this year and the first trimester of 2021. For this purpose, further lockdowns are planned, which will be officially justified by a supposed second and third wave of the pandemic. You are well aware of the means that have been deployed to sow panic and legitimize draconian limitations on individual liberties, artfully provoking a world-wide economic crisis. In the intentions of the architects, this crisis will serve to make the recourse of nations to the *Great Reset* irreversible, thereby giving the final blow to a world whose existence and very memory they want to completely cancel. But this world, Mr. President, includes people, affections, institutions, faith, culture, traditions, and ideals: people and values that do not act like automatons, who do not obey like machines, because they are endowed with a soul and a heart, because they are tied together by a spiritual bond that draws its strength from above, from that God that our adversaries want to challenge, just as Lucifer did at the beginning of time with his *"non serviam."*

Many people - as we well know - are annoyed by this reference to the clash between Good and Evil and the use of "apocalyptic" overtones, which according to them exasperates spirits and sharpens divisions. It is not surprising that the enemy is angered at being discovered just when he believes he has reached the citadel he seeks to conquer undisturbed. What is surprising, however, is that there is no one to sound the alarm. The reaction of the deep state to those who denounce its plans is broken and incoherent, but understandable. Just when the complicity of the mainstream media had succeeded in making the transition to the New World Oder almost painless and unnoticed, all sorts of deceptions, scandals and crimes are coming to light.

Until a few months ago, it was easy to smear as "conspiracy theorists" those who denounced these terrible plans, which we now see are being carried out down to the smallest detail. No one, up until last February, would ever have thought that, in all of our cities, citizens would be arrested simply for wanting to walk down the street, to breathe, to want to keep their business open, to want to go to church on Sunday. Yet now it is happening all over the world, even in picture-postcard Italy that many Americans consider to be a small enchanted country, with its ancient monuments, its churches, its charming cities, its characteristic villages. And while the politicians are barricaded inside their palaces promulgating decrees like Persian satraps, businesses are failing, shops are closing, and people are prevented from living, traveling, working and praying. The disastrous psychological consequences of this operation are already being seen, beginning with the suicides of desperate entrepreneurs and of our children, segregated from friends and classmates, and told to follow their classes while sitting at home alone in front of a computer.

In Sacred Scripture, Saint Paul speaks to us of "the one who opposes" the manifestation of the *mystery of iniquity*, the *kathèkon* (2 Thess. 2:6-7). In the religious sphere, this obstacle to evil is the Church, and in particular the papacy; in the political sphere, it is those who impede the establishment of the New World Order.

As is now clear, the one who occupies the Chair of Peter has betrayed his role from the very beginning in order to defend and promote the globalist ideology, supporting the agenda of the deep church, who chose him from its ranks.

Mr. President, you have already clearly stated that you want to defend the nation - *One Nation under God*, fundamental liberties, and non-negotiable values that are denied and fought against today. It is you, dear President, who are "the one who opposes" the deep state, the final assault of the children of darkness.

For this reason, it is necessary that all people of good will be persuaded of the epochal importance of the imminent election: not so much for the sake of this or that political program, but because of the general inspiration of your action that best embodies - in this particular historical context - that world, our world, which they want to cancel by means of the lockdown. Your adversary is also our adversary; it is the Enemy of the human race, He who is "a murderer from the beginning" (Jn 8:44).

Around you are gathered with faith and courage those who consider you the final garrison against the world dictatorship. The alternative is to vote for a person who is manipulated by the deep state, gravely compromised by scandals and corruption, who will do to the United States what Jorge Mario Bergoglio is doing to the Church, Prime Minister Conte to Italy, President Macron to France, Prime Minister

Sanchez to Spain, and so on. The blackmailable nature of Joe Biden - just like that of the prelates of the Vatican's "magic circle" - will expose him to be used unscrupulously, allowing illegitimate powers to interfere in both domestic politics as well as international balances. It is obvious that those who manipulate him already have someone worse than him ready, with whom they will replace him as soon as the opportunity arises.

And yet, in the midst of this bleak picture, this apparently unstoppable advance of the "Invisible Enemy," an element of hope emerges. The adversary does not know how to love, and it does not understand that it is not enough to assure a universal income or to cancel mortgages in order to subjugate the masses and convince them to be branded like cattle. This people, which for too long has endured the abuses of a hateful and tyrannical power, is rediscovering that it has a soul; it is understanding that it is not willing to exchange its freedom for the homogenization and cancellation of its identity; it is beginning to understand the value of familial and social ties, of the bonds of faith and culture that unite honest people. This *Great Reset* is destined to fail because those who planned it do not understand that there are still people ready to take to the streets to defend their rights, to protect their loved ones, to give a future to their children and grandchildren. The leveling inhumanity of the globalist project will shatter miserably in the face of the firm and courageous opposition of the children of Light. The enemy has Satan on its side, He who only knows how to hate. But on our side, we have the Lord Almighty, the God of armies arrayed for battle, and the Most Holy Virgin, who will crush the head of the Ancient Serpent. "If God is for us, who can be against us?" (Rom 8:31).

Mr. President, you are well aware that, in this crucial hour, the United States of America is considered the defending wall against which the war declared by the advocates of globalism has been unleashed. Place your trust in the Lord, strengthened by the word of the Apostle Paul: "I can do all things in Him who strengthens me" (Phil 4:13). To be an instrument of Divine Providence is a great responsibility, for which you will certainly receive all the graces of state that you need, since they are being fervently implored for you by the many people who support you with their prayers.

With this heavenly hope and assurance of my prayer for you, for the First Lady, and for your collaborators, with all my heart I send you my blessing.

God bless the United States of America!

+ Carlo Maria Viganò
Tit. Archbishop of Ulpiana
Former Apostolic Nuncio to the United States of America"[5]

From the insightful words of these courageous and articulate spokesmen and watchmen on the wall there can be no doubt that America and the world are on the brink of a cataclysm of unprecedented biblical proportions which are described in the prophecies of Revelation 6:12-14 and Matthew 24:29 which we have been examining together here in this chapter. Consequently, if this is true, and it is, the logical thing to do would be to read the Bible verses which immediately follow these two Bible passages to understand what we can expect to follow these present times in the very near future. Here are those two passages:

> *"And the kings of the earth, and the great men, and the rich men, and the chief captains, and the mighty men, and every bondman, and every free man, hid themselves in the dens and in the rocks of the mountains; And said to the mountains and rocks, Fall on us, and hide us from the face of him that sitteth on the throne (namely God or YHWH), and from the wrath of the Lamb (Yahushua): For the great day of his wrath is come; and who shall be able to stand?"* Revelation 6:15-17

> *"And then shall appear the sign of the Son of man (Yahushua) in heaven: and then shall all the tribes of the earth mourn, and they shall see the Son of man coming in the clouds of heaven with power and great glory. And he shall send his angels with*

---

[5] https://qanon.pub, Post #4941 dated Oct. 30, 2020.

a great sound of a trumpet, and they shall gather together his elect from the four winds, from one end of heaven to the other." Matthew 24:30-31

Both of these passages are describing different aspects of Yahushua's long awaited second coming on the great, terrible and last day of the Lord, in which Yahushua will gather the resurrected and transformed elect to Himself in the clouds and then tread the winepress of the fierceness and wrath of almighty God (see Revelation 19:15) upon the wicked and the foolish non-elect vessels of dishonor who remain on earth after the gathering of the elect to Himself. From my observations and analysis, it appears that roughly 9,999 out of every 10,000 people alive on earth today comprises this latter group of people.

This analysis is not rocket science. It's rather straightforward. However, we are dealing with an imminent event in world history which will result in the violent and horrible deaths of almost all the 7.8 billion people alive on earth today which rightly frighten most people and torment the demons which afflict them to no end. For anyone to face their imminent end head on would inevitably drive those people insane. So instead, they play pretend and willfully ignore all the compelling evidence I have laid out here of what's soon coming upon them. Furthermore, YHWH, in His mercy, has sent strong delusion upon every one of the poor souls, so that they would believe one or more lies and remain relatively clueless about what's really coming until that day arrives. Here's the proof text for this finding:

"And with all deceivableness of unrighteousness in them that perish; because they received not the love of the truth, that they might be saved. And for this cause God (Eloah) shall send them strong delusion, that they should believe a lie: That they all might be damned who believed not the truth, but had pleasure in unrighteousness." 2 Thessalonians 2:10-12.

This already fulfilled prophecy fully explains why so few people are to this day awake and fully aware of the existence, actions and agenda of the global elite conspiracy of Satan worshippers who rule our world today through the exercise of their occult demon spirit powers over the rest of us. Even more, it reveals why the vast majority of humanity alive on earth today cannot see what is inevitably coming right behind this global tyranny that directly impacts their eternal destinities.

4. The Significance of the 2020 Presidential Election

It is now over two months since the November 3, 2020 fake Presidential selection of our puppet-in-chief for the next four years. As of this writing, no winner has been legally declared, just as Paul Craig Roberts predicted, and for the reasons he articulated in the recent article he wrote in the *American Free Press,* which I quoted from in Chapter 3 of this book. It appears that the Democrats have employed sophisticated software weaponry, developed and deployed by the CIA against foreign governments that the American military/security complex wanted to topple, against the American people and the American constitutional republic in this fraudulent election. The rule of law is all but dead in our nation. Lawlessness on steroids is what most accurately describes American political processes and life in America today and it will never improve, because Satan, the god of this world, is on his last legs and is desperate to inflict as much injury upon humanity and the decent as he possibly can before YHWH tosses him, along with the first beast of the global elite conspiracy, and the false prophet and second beast of all forms of false organized religion, into the burning lake of fire and brimstone for all eternity as YHWH promises us He will do in Revelation 20:10:

> *"And the devil that deceived them was cast into the lake of fire and brimstone, where the beast and the false prophet are, and shall be tormented day and night for ever and ever."*

Americans have been presented with a choice between two moral deviants to choose between: Donald Trump and Mike Pence, of the Republican Party or Joe Biden and Kamala Harris of the Democrat Party. Both teams are equally beholden to the same group of puppet masters who make up the leadership of the Council of Foreign Relations (CFR), the most publicly visible arm of the Satan-worshipping Illuminati in America since its founding in 1921 by Rothschild agent, Col. Edward Mandel House. The illusion of choice is a fraud of monumental proportions. American politicians consistently lie and promise the voters whatever they think will get them the most votes, only to do whatever the puppet masters who pull their strings tell them to do once they are in office. Have you noticed that the foreign and domestic policy decisions of consecutive Democrat and Republican administrations do not materially differ from one another? This is all by design of The Powers That Be, the east coast Establishment, the Illuminati and Freemasonry, and the devil they all serve.

From today's vantage point, it is fairly easy to see that Donald Trump, the actor and television star of the TV show, *The Apprentice*, and New York real estate tycoon and playboy, was tapped decades ago by the Rothschild banking dynasty, whose agent, Wilbur Ross, bailed Trump out of bankruptcy in 1992. It really does not take a genius to deduce that the Rothschilds chose to invest in Donald Trump in order to install him as their latest puppet in the White House in 2016. All the polls were manufactured and manipulated to cause the American public to believe that Hillary Clinton was a virtual shoo-in for the presidency in 2016, only to be surprised the night of the selection with Trump being declared the winner of a rigged, fraudulent and fake election, as they all are. And let us not forget: while the global elite conspiracy clearly chose Donald Trump as their "administrator" in the White House, YHWH, the Grand Director of this entire play, was orchestrating everything toward this result as well. Because nothing happens outside of the sovereign will of almighty YHWH or God.

Donald Trump is a wealthy billionaire, a charlatan, a snake oil salesman, a pathological liar, and a vain and godless man who has kept the company of some very seedy characters over his adult life including the Jewish Mafia sodomite lawyer Roy Cohn, pedophile sex compromise operator Jeffrey Epstein, moral deviants and pathological liars Hillary and Bill Clinton and corrupt Israeli Prime Minister, Benjamin Netanyahu, to name some of the most egregious examples. Trump is also an unabashed and enthusiastic Zionist and advocate for the Ashkenazi Talmudic Jews of New York City who have financed his career and his flashy playboy lifestyle. Until rather recently, Trump was a member of and contributor to the Democratic Party. These are the hard facts that Trump supporters choose to overlook, dismiss or ignore, but they are no less the facts because they choose to ignore or deny them.

Trump, now 74, has marketed himself as a skillful businessman, the defender of free market capitalism and American nationalism and a champion fighting against globalism, socialism and the New World Order. His political supporters, who mainly identify themselves as political, economic and social conservatives, American patriots, Tea Partiers, and Christian Zionists (an oxymoron if there ever was one) are usually swept up in a flood of unfounded hero worship for this very flawed man.

Trump's running mate, Mike Pence, is an unabashed Zionist hawk. He claims to be an evangelical Catholic, which is an oxymoron; however, people in our culture are so ignorant on so many subjects that Pence gets away with this deception. What is most troubling is that during the 2016 Presidential campaign, a Tory Smith recorded and posted several YouTube videos in one of which he claimed that as of May 29, 2016, Indiana Governor (at the time) Mike Pence had raped 186 children and that he had murdered 54 of them.[6]

Wayne Madsen, in his Wayne Madsen Report, reports six instances he has uncovered in which Donald Trump paid fairly large legal settlements totaling roughly $40 million to six minors (3 females and 3 males), ages 10 to 13, whom Madsen has alleged Trump raped from 1989 to 2012.[7] If these

---

6 https://www.youtube.com/watchj?v=P9WKL_UNxds. Tory Smith. May 29, 2016.

7 *Why is Trump so afraid of Cohen's testimony?* https://www.waynemadsenreport.com. January 14-15, 2019.

allegations concerning Mike Pence and Donald Trump are true, which they quite likely are, we can be quite certain that these two men are demon-possessed psychopaths who are fully compromised and easily blackmailed by their globalist puppet masters. Sadly, this appears to be how the game of hardball, high stakes politics in America is played by all those who wield substantial political power and influence in this country.

Trump's opponent in 2020 is Joe Biden, a 47-year long career politician from Baltimore, Maryland (originally from Scranton, Pennsylvania) who served as President Barack Obama's Vice President from 2008 to 2016. Biden is 77 years old, has been caught on video repeatedly sniffing women's and little girl's hair and touching them inappropriately. For these seriously deviant behaviors, he has deservedly acquired the nickname of "Creepy Uncle Joe Biden." Furthermore, there are a number of allegations made by women over Biden's career that he has forced himself sexually upon them, which the lying mainstream media has effectively silenced and suppressed, but it is quite likely that most, if not all, of the allegations of his sexual misconduct are true.

During the latter days of the Presidential campaign, emails and videos concerning Biden's son, Hunter Biden, emerged which strongly indicated that Biden, his brother Jim and his son Hunter sold political favors to Russian, Ukrainian and Chinese oligarchs and the Chinese Communist Party for substantial bribes and other payments that Joe Biden personally took a cut of. Such conduct on Biden's part amounts to racketeering, bribery and treason.

Biden's performance on the campaign trail was underwhelming, to say the least. He exhibited behavior that seems to indicate that he is suffering from some form of early stage dementia, although I suspect that it is far more indicative of the confounding effects of the demon spirits which possess and control him, than anything else.

The policy positions Biden claimed he advocates are as blatantly in furtherance of the New World Order globalist agenda as can possibly be imagined. These policy positions include advocating for the radical and dangerous Green New Deal and the phasing out of the oil industry, confiscating Americans' guns, opening our borders to unlimited illegal immigration, stacking the courts, raising taxes substantially and imposing mandatory nationwide Covid lockdowns. Moreover, Biden was foolish enough to allow himself to be caught on video boasting in front of the Council on Foreign Relations of how he withheld $1 billion of foreign aid to the Ukraine unless and until the President of the Ukraine fired the special prosecutor looking into the suspicious and likely corrupt dealings of his son Hunter Biden who was receiving unjustifiably large payments for serving on the board of directors of energy company, Burisma Holdings, controlled by a well-known and corrupt Ukrainian oligarch who sought access to Vice President Joe Biden. Biden was boasting to the CFR of his prowess as a shakedown artist and as an extortionist. He was equally foolish to allow himself to be filmed on video openly admitting to the Democrats of having assembled "the largest and most inclusive voter fraud organization in the history of American politics" in connection with his campaign for President this year.[8]

Biden's running mate, Kamala Harris, is equally concerning to most Americans. It seems quite apparent that Biden has been instructed to select Harris as his running mate and that if elected, Biden will voluntarily turn over the reins of power to his Vice President and step down as President, likely triggering a globalist, Communist takeover of America and its institutions by the wantonly corrupt and Marxist Democrat Party. Harris is a dangerous and unprincipled opportunist and tyrant, who would inevitably create anger and division in America if she were ever entrusted with real political power.

As of this writing, a number of states' elections are being challenged by the Trump campaign, which is alleging substantial evidence of election fraud, that from everything I have read and researched, seems well founded. Meanwhile, the

---

[8] Greg Hunter - Weekly News Wrap-Up 11.06.2020. *https://www.youtube.com/watch?v=C1DWrkVn_s4.*

lying legacy media has presumptively declared Joe Biden to be the President-Elect, which it is not the media's role to declare, especially in light of the extensive number of lawsuits that have been filed to date or which are in the process of being filed, contesting the election results and counting processes in the states of Georgia, Pennsylvania, Michigan, Wisconsin, Arizona and Nevada.

I watched the election night report of Greg Hunter on his YouTube channel, USAWatchdog.com, until about midnight, EST, on the night of November 3, 2020. You can go back and view the same reporting I witnessed using the footnoted link below.[9] In it, Greg was modeling a map of electoral college votes earned by both candidates, based on the percentages of votes being reported by FOX News as having been counted and the gap in the number of votes by which each candidate was ahead or behind in each state. Under the most optimistic of assumptions for Biden, he was coming out with only 240 electoral votes versus 298 electoral votes going to Trump, where 270 electoral votes are needed to win the fabricated contest. The more likely outcome was headed toward about 311 electoral votes for Trump and about 227 electoral votes for Biden. In short, Trump was winning decisively and by a landslide, just as I have been predicting would inevitably happen for months. Recently, I have seen estimates that the number of electoral college votes which Trump should have earned may be as high as 410 v. 175 for Biden.

There are a number of reports indicating that the Trump campaign was fully anticipating and was prepared to document extensive voting and election fraud planned by the Democrats and the Biden campaign. As mentioned previously, Biden was so reckless and over-confident that he freely admitted on camera before the election that his campaign had assembled "the most extensive and inclusive voter fraud organization in the history of American politics." You just cannot make this stuff up! It is simply unbelievable and proves how depraved

---

[9] https://www.youtube.com/watch?v=YLj49WmCzAs. Greg Hunter. Nov. 4, 2020

and wicked our entire culture has now become, such that it tolerates this overt and reckless lawlessness and criminality from the criminal psychopaths running for the office of the President of the United States. But for those of you paying attention, this really should come as no surprise to any of us, in light of the admission made in the *Protocols of the Learned Elders of Zion* some 125 years ago:

> "For a time, until there will no longer be any risk in entrusting responsible posts in our States to our brother-Jews, we shall put them in the hands of persons whose past and reputation are such that between them and the people lies an abyss, persons who, in case of disobedience to our instructions, must face criminal charges or disappear - this in order to make them defend our interests to their last gasp." [10]

The Talmudic fake Jews (the synagogue of Satan of Revelation 2:9 and 3:9) who rule our world today were broadcasting in 1895 that they would, in time, make a complete mockery of the gentile nations and their leaders by ensuring that the puppets they placed in power, including America's Presidents, would be totally compromised and blackmailed by these evil cretins. The same conclusion can be made about Trump and Pence as can be made about Biden and Harris. They are all crooks and thugs, who do the bidding of their globalist luciferian puppet masters, who pull all their strings outside of the purview of the American public and with the full support and complicity of the lying mainstream media, all six conglomerates of which the Talmudic Ashkenazi Jews of the world own and control lock, stock and barrel.

But let us not forget that YHWH, the God of the KJV Bible, the Grand Director of his huge, complex and multi-faceted play, remains fully in control over all world events down to the most minute of details. Therefore, if we fail to remember this simple fact, which most people have no clue about, we run the risk of despairing and losing all hope. But armed with this

---

[10] *Protocols of the Meetings of the Learned Elders of Zion.* Protocol No. 8, paragraph 5, p. 25.

insight and knowledge, we can take a rather detached view of the entire mess that we Americans are now witnessing and realize that however this play unfolds, God is telling a few of us, His elect, what really matters, and what does not. The global elites, who practice the dark arts of the occult and who engage in all sorts of perverted sex acts with children that have the effect of possessing them with powerful demon spirits which give them substantial temporal powers over others, and along with it wealth, fame and status in the world, are incapable of seeing, perceiving and understanding this greater objective, absolute reality:

> *"The wicked, through the pride of his countenance, will not seek after God (Elohim): God (Elohim) is not in all his thoughts. His ways are always grievous;* **thy judgments are far above out of his sight***: as for all his enemies, he puffeth at them. He hath said in his heart, I shall not be moved: for I shall never be in adversity."* Psalm 10:4-6 (Bold face added for emphasis)

So when we look at the American Presidential contest that is underway right now from a ten thousand foot elevation vantage point, the strategic thinker can see that since God is fully in control of all things, and that absolutely nothing happens outside of His sovereign will, and since all of us have no control over the outcome of this fully rigged and corrupt process, the resolution of the dispute is going to reveal to us some important truths which YHWH wishes to reveal to the few of us who are of His born again elect. I really don't know who will ultimately be declared the winner of this meaningless public contest and I really don't care what the outcome of it is. Because either way, YHWH, the Grand Director of His play, is flawlessly executing and directing His predestinated plan for His ultimate glory. I just want whatever He wills, without exception. To oppose YHWH in anything is a fool's errand and quite hopeless. So I don't go there any longer. I know better now.

What we have known since about April of this year is that if Trump is declared the winner of this contest, in whatever way it ultimately plays itself out, that Biden will never concede the election to Trump, and that the Democrat Party leadership in America will function as demagogues to incite the demon-possessed mob of the political left to burn American cities to the ground in a well-planned and orchestrated Marxist takeover of America in a Communist coup or civil war that is likely to turn violent and bloody, very quickly. How the well-armed and well-equipped patriotic political right will respond to this reign of terror, reminiscent of the the reign of terror of the French Revolution in 1789, in which three million Frenchmen lost their heads to the guillotine at the hands of the drug-induced demonic mob of those days, fueled by the planned demagoguery of Freemasons and the Illuminati, is a big unknown to everyone. We shall know very soon, because this day is fast approaching us and there is no way to stop it, because the global elite conspiracy of Satan worshippers is desperate and now fully out in the open pushing their demonic agendas in public. It is now do or die for all of them, and they clearly know it.

What is very clear to me is that YHWH will not permit anyone to eclipse His glory. So at some point very soon, He is likely to step onto the stage of His own play in a very dramatic way, most likely in the form of the sudden and quite unexpected return of His son, Yahushua, in the clouds with power and great glory to gather the elect to Himself and to then tread the winepress of the fierceness and wrath of almighty God (YHWH) upon the wicked and the foolish who remain behind. When this occurs, and it now appears that all the pieces are arrayed on the chessboard for it to happen quite soon, it will be the grand climax to all of world history: His story!

I cannot have this discussion today with anyone who does not number among God's born again elect. The vast majority of people that I encounter when I mention aspects of this just stare back at me in silence with blank looks on their faces. They have nothing to say. I have seen it now countless times and it is just eerie to witness. It just proves to me that the entirety of the KJV Bible is 100% trustworthy, reliable and true, and that nothing else is. But tell that to a strongly deluded wicked fool who has been wrongly taught all his or her life that the Bible is just a book of fairy tales written by ignorant and primitive goat and sheep herders that has been changed and re-written countless times in the past. It is pointless to argue with willfully ignorant and wicked fools who have no interest in the truth. Wisdom says, just walk away. They'll never understand and never believe it anyway.

What is interesting and quite instructive to observe is how easily the masses of humanity in America have become brain washed and deceived by the political left v. right divide and conquer ploy that the global elites and world leaders have been using to manipulate and control their subjects since the beginning of world history, pitting both groups against one another, to divert their attention from the rampant theft and criminality of the ruling oligarchy of secret society thugs and demon-possessed psychopaths, whom the lying media they own and control exalt as gods that we all ought to be swooning over. It's really a very clever and devious ploy, when you think about it properly this way.

The simple truth of the matter is that all politicians are professional and skillful liars with one or more embarrassing and career-ending indiscretions in their pasts that the global elite puppet masters know all about and use to control their puppets to do their bidding to their last gasp, as the *Protocols* so delicately put it. Place your trust in any politician and you have placed your trust and faith in a useless idol, is what God is telling all of us by this mess He is now revealing to all of us. Trump and Biden should merely be viewed as two Mafia dons, representing different organized crime syndicates, both of whom serve the devil, who are fighting with each other for dominance over something that is swiftly perishing and will soon be utterly worthless.

Nevertheless, YHWH has used the fake political drama in America in 2020, and now 2021, to set things up for one of three outcomes. He either is planning to permit Trump to be declared the winner of a contested selection process, which will be met with widescale violence and destruction in American cities from the political left, over which YHWH may or may not permit Trump to declare martial law, or He will permit

Trump to be declared the winner, and before the violence and mayhem begins, He will send His son Yahushua back in His second coming, to pre-empt everything else.

A third possibility is that America's courts, other legal institutions and the U.S. Congress are so corrupt and deceitful that they permit Joe Biden to be inaugurated as President on January 20, but I view this possible outcome as extremely unlikely, inasmuch as it is quite obvious to me what YHWH is now up to, based on the words of a number of the psalms with which I am very familiar. Those psalms call upon and describe God confounding the wicked, shaming and disgracing them quite publicly by exposing and revealing their lawless and criminal acts of wickedness right before He destroys them. His allowing Biden and the lying and duplicitous mainstream media to steal this election would largely defeat those divine, biblical and prophetic purposes. This is why I regard this third possible outcome as the least likely of the three options.

Frankly speaking, and I am speculating here, not making a firm prediction, I think the second course of action, in which Trump is declared the winner and the second coming happens before the violence and mayhem begins, is far more in keeping with YHWH's nature as revealed to us in His stories of the Bible in the Old Testament. YHWH repeats Himself in some rather distinct and predictable patterns throughout history. The looming calamity of Trump being declared the winner and the Marxist, Democrat political leftists being on the brink of erupting in violence, mayhem and destruction is very much analogous to the time when Moses and the Israelites were fleeing from Egypt and Pharaoh and his Egyptian army were pursuing them to slaughter all of them on the shores of the Gulf of Aqaba of the Red Sea. What looked like certain slaughter of the nation and the twelve tribes of Israel at the hands of the Egyptians, turned out to be an amazing miracle of redemption and reversal as Moses spread his staff over the waters of the Red Sea, YHWH parted the waters, the Israelites walked across a dry land bridge to the other side of the Gulf of Aqaba onto what is today Saudi Arabia, and then YHWH released the walls of water He had been holding back and drowned all of Pharaoh's pursuing army, in which not one Egyptian was left alive.

And who got all the glory, honor and praise for this divine miracle? YHWH did, of course. In like manner, if all the violence and mayhem of the political left in America was halted by the second coming of Yahushua, in which the righteous are gathered to Himself and the wicked and the foolish are annihilated for all time, who would get all the glory for it? YHWH and Yahushua would, of course. Because of its potential for high drama and God's maximum glory, I'm betting that this scenario is the one that YHWH is most likely going to orchestrate and direct in the very near future.

The first scenario is plausible as well, as Trump's declaration of martial law would serve as a signal to the global elites to go hide in their underground bunkers, thus fulfilling the prophecy of Revelation 6:15-17 perfectly. But today, we are seeing the global elite fraudsters claiming a resurgence of Covid cases that they are responding to with more stringent lockdowns and closures of businesses and schools. These lockdown measures could serve as the signal for the elites to go hide in their underground bunkers in lieu of a declaration of martial law by Trump. Either way, we know that the elites have to go hide in their underground bunkers before the second coming of Yahushua can occur. That much is certain, since all scripture, when fulfilled, is always fulfilled perfectly and completely and Revelation 6:15-17 have yet to happen, that the Bible reveals must precede the second coming of Yahushua.

5. Is the Climax and Conclusion to YHWH's Play Now Just Around the Corner?

In these final days of these end times, the monstrous hoax and fraud of the alleged Covid pestilence which, if it exists it all, is a U.S. government funded bio weapon turned on the citizens of the world, and more recently the overt and monstrous voting and election fraud of the November 3, 2020 Presidential election in the sharply divided United States, when combined together, present a complex jigsaw puzzle and picture in which multiple forces are heading toward a cataclysm of monstrous and biblical proportions that is both undeniable and inescapable. What events and results are we likely to witness in the coming weeks and months? To begin with, we must go back to the script that the Grand Director is clearly working off of that consists of end times Bible prophecy and see what it has to say and teach us.

In Chapter 3, I revealed the evidence for why it is quite likely that the events described in Matthew 24:29 and Revelation 6:12-14 have recently occurred, both of which describe the same prophesied event in slightly different, but eerily similar, metaphorical language. And on page 80, I lay out the passages of Matthew 24:30-31 and Revelation 6:15-17 which describe the biblical events which YHWH has revealed will shortly follow that which has already occurred that will result in the second coming of Yahushua the Messiah in His long-awaited return and climax to God's story and all of world history.

5. Is the Climax and Conclusion to YHWH's Play Now Just Around the Corner?

What exactly can we expect to occur in this second coming of Yahushua? Let's let the three most descriptive texts in scripture tell us, in YHWH's own inspired and infallible words:

> *"And then shall appear the Son of man in heaven: and then shall all the tribes of the earth mourn, and they shall see the Son of man (Yahushua) coming in the clouds of heaven with power and great glory. And he shall send his angels with a great sound of a trumpet, and they shall gather together his elect from the four winds, from one end of heaven to another."* Matthew 24:30-31

> *"But I would not have you to be ignorant, brethren, concerning them which are asleep (have already died in Christ), that ye sorrow not, even as others which have no hope. For if we believe that Jesus (Yahushua) died and rose again, even so them also which sleep in Jesus (Yahushua) will God (Eloah) bring with him. For this we say unto you by the the word of the Lord, that we which are alive and remain unto the coming of the Lord shall not prevent them which are asleep (shall not prevent those who have already died in Christ from being resurrected). For the Lord himself shall descend from heaven with a shout, with the voice of the archangel, and with the trump of God (Eloah): and the dead in Christ (the Messiah) shall rise (be resurrected from their graves and ascend first into the sky to be with Yahushua): Then we which are alive and remain shall be caught up together with them in the clouds to meet the Lord in the air: and so shall we ever be with the Lord."* 1 Thessalonians 4:13-17 (Parentheticals added for clarity)

> *"Behold, I shew you a mystery; We shall not all sleep (die), but we shall all be changed (transformed), In a moment, in the twinkling of an eye, at the last trump: for the trumpet shall sound, and the dead shall be raised incorruptible (raised from their graves and resurrected in physical bodies like the resurrected body of Yahushua), and we shall be changed (transformed). For this corruptible (aging, decaying body) must put on incorruption (a physical body that does not grow old and decay), and this mortal (body) must put on immortality (a body*

> *that never dies). So when this corruptible (body) shall have put on incorruption, and this mortal (body) shall have put on immortality, then shall be brought to pass the saying that is written, Death is swallowed up in victory. O death, where is they sting? O grave, where is thy victory?"* 1 Corinthians 15:51-55 (Parentheticals added for clarity)

Thus, simply put, all of God's born again elect adopted sons and daughters of God, through faith in His son, Yahushua, will receive new immortal, resurrected bodies, just as happened to Yahushua the Messiah nearly 2000 years ago after He was in the grave for three days after His crucifixion, in which He paid the price we deserved to pay for our sins we have committed, so that His righteousness might be imputed or credited to us.

Following this climactic event, scripture tells us that we will then become part of a great multitude before the throne of God and before Yahushua, clothed in white robes, signifying righteousness, with palm branches in our hands and praising and worshipping God the Father and God the Son in heaven in Revelation 7:9-10:

> *"After this I beheld, and lo, a great multitude, which no man could number, of all nations, and kindreds, and people, and tongues, stood before the throne (of God or YHWH), and before the Lamb (Yahushua), clothed with white robes, and palms in their hands; And cried with a loud voice, saying Salvation to our God (Eloah) which sitteth upon the throne and unto the Lamb."* (Parentheticals added for clarity)

Shortly thereafter (scripture is silent as to how long, but not long), we are told that a marriage supper of the Lamb (Yahushua) will occur in heaven between Yahushua the Messiah, the spiritual bridegroom and His church, the body of true believers, His spiritual bride, in Revelation 19:7-9:

> *"Let us be glad and rejoice, and give honour to him: for the marriage of the Lamb (Yahushua) is come, and his wife (his elect, resurrected bride, his community of believers in Him) hath made herself ready. And to her was granted that she should be arrayed in fine linen, clean and white: for the fine linen is the righteousness of saints (the born again elect). And he saith unto*

> *me, Write, Blessed are they which are called unto the marriage supper of the Lamb. And he saith unto me, These are the true sayings of God (Eloah)."* (Parentheticals added for clarity)

Immediately following this passage, we read of the return of Yahushua to earth to make war against the kings of the earth and their armies, led by the first beast and the false prophet (the second beast) foretold in Revelation 13. It is not the least bit a fair fight: the armies of the earth are totally annihilated in what is commonly referred to as the Battle of Armageddon. It tells a story of horrific destruction and death of the rulers (the global elite conspiracy) and their armies of this foul and wicked world:

> *"And I saw heaven opened, and behold a white horse; and he that sat upon him was called Faithful and True (Yahushua the Messiah, King of Kings and Lord of lords), and in righteousness he doth judge and make war (against the wicked). His eyes were as a flame of fire, and on his head were many crowns; and he had a name written, that no man knew, but he himself. And he was clothed with a vesture dipped in blood: and his name is called The Word of God (Eloah -see John 1:1-3 for an explanation of this reference). And the armies which were in heaven followed him upon white horses, clothed in fine linen, white and clean (these are the same people who are described above in the marriage supper of the Lamb - all of us who number among the resurrected, born again, elect saints). And out of his mouth goeth a sharp sword, that with it he should smite the nations: and he shall rule them with a rod of iron:* ***and he treadeth the winepress of the fierceness and wrath of Almighty God*** *(Eloah). And he hath on his vesture and on his thigh a name written, KING OF KINGS AND LORD OF LORDS."* Revelation 19:11-16

In this passage, we can see that Yahushua the Messiah is by no means returning meek and mild to wage war with the first beast, the kings of the earth and their armies and the false prophet. He is more powerful than (and separate from) His entire creation, which He created, and the ruler of the entire earth and He plans to return to destroy the rulers and forces of evil once and for all for all eternity. The passage describes a fearsome sight of unlimited power and might in the person of Yahushua (Christ). Now the passage describes the Battle of Armageddon that is not the least bit a fair fight:

> *"And I saw an angel standing in the sun; and he cried with a loud voice, saying to all the fowls that fly in the midst of heaven, Come and gather yourselves together unto the supper of the great God (Eloah); That ye may eat the flesh of kings, and the flesh of captains, and the flesh of mighty men, and the flesh of horses, and of them that sit on them, and the flesh of all men, both free and bond, both small and great (all of whom are wicked fools who are at enmity with God). And I saw the beast, and the kings of the earth, and their armies (the global elite conspiracy and their minions), gathered together to make war against him that sat on the horse (Yahushua) and against his army (of His resurrected elect). And the beast (the global elite economic and political conspiracy) was taken, and with him the false prophet (all forms of organized and false religion, led by the abomination of the Roman Catholic Church) that wrought miracles (occult magic spells) before him, with which he deceived them that had received the mark of the beast, and them that worshipped his image (swore allegiance and loyalty to the globalist beast system).* **These both were cast alive into a lake burning with brimstone**. *And the remnant were slain with the sword of him that sat upon the horse, which sword (the word of God) proceeded out of his mouth: and all the fouls were filled with their flesh."* Revelation 19:17-21 (Parentheticals added for clarity; bold face added for emphasis)

Immediately following this passage of prophecy, the Apostle John reveals to us yet another vision with a much broader time horizon, which dates back to the crucifixion of Yahushua, nearly 2000 years ago and ends around the same time as the vision which we just finished reading together. Yahushua tells us in John 12:31 that the devil, the prince of this world, would be cast out of heaven, with His death upon the cross:

5. Is the Climax and Conclusion to YHWH's Play Now Just Around the Corner?

"Now is the judgment of this world: now shall the prince of this world (the devil) be cast out." (Parenthetical added for clarity)

With this understanding and context, the timeline of the following passage becomes much more clear:

"And I saw an angel come down from heaven (Yahushua or Christ), having the key of the bottomless pit and a great chain in his hand. And he laid hold on the dragon, that old serpent, which is the Devil, and Satan, and bound him a thousand years, And cast him into the bottomless it, and shut him up, and set a seal upon him, that he should deceive the nations no more, till the thousand years should be fulfilled: and after that he must be loosed a little season." Revelation 20:1-3

Now obviously, no literal pit can be bottomless, can it? So clearly the pit that the devil was cast into was a metaphor for a very deep pit, but not literally a bottomless one. In a similar fashion, Chapter 20 of the Book of Revelation makes reference to a thousand years ***SIX*** times! This should be viewed as a huge red flag that it should not be understood literally, but figuratively, as meaning a very long time or a very large number. For example, we are told by YHWH in Psalm 50:10, *"for every beast of the forest is mine, and the cattle upon a thousand hills."* If this verse is to be understood literally, then who owns the cattle on all the remaining hills? So obviously, in this instance, a thousand means a large number and is not properly understood literally as one thousand hills. It's like the expression, "thanks a million." The same reasoning applies to the six references to a thousand years in Revelation 20: it means a long time; close to a literal 2000 years in fact, we can now deduce from the time which has passed since Yahushua's death on the cross in 31 A.D.

Returning to the passage above, we know from referring back to John 12:31 that the devil was cast into a metaphorical pit upon Christ's death on the cross. The little season in which the devil would be loosed is a reference to the season in which the first beast of Revelation 13 is granted his power to wreak havoc on the earth, which the prophet Daniel appears to be describing as the three and a half year or 1,290 day great tribulation of Daniel 12:7 and 12:11, respectively. The Apostle John continues:

> *"And I saw thrones, and they sat upon them, and judgment was given unto them: and I saw the souls of them that were beheaded (martyred) for the witness of Jesus (Yahushua), and for the word of God (Eloah), and which had not worshipped the beast, neither his image, neither had received his mark upon their foreheads or in their hands; and they lived and reigned with Christ (the Messiah) a thousand years."* Revelation 20:4

Now exactly when was this metaphorical kingdom set up? For most theologians who have been trained in seminaries over the last one hundred years, they will wrongly tell you that the thousand years is to be understood literally, not figuratively, and that it would not begin until the second coming of Christ occurs and that His followers would reign with Him on earth for a literal one thousand years. Where on earth do they come up with such a preposterous and absurd notion? From the crooked lawyer, Freemason and Jew Cyrus Ingerson Scofield, author of the Scofield Reference Bible of 1909, who first advanced these deliberately false and misleading teachings to lead people astray, to their eternal harm and damnation, if that were possible. Thankfully, it's not. So what is the truth?

Daniel 2:44 provides us with our answer:

> *"And in the days of these kings (the four empires ending with the Roman Empire) shall the God (Elah) of heaven set up a kingdom (the kingdom of Christ in heaven), which shall never be destroyed: and the kingdom shall not be left to other people, but it shall break in pieces and consume all these kingdoms and it shall stand forever."* (Parentheticals added for clarity)

Revelation 20 continues,

> *"But the rest of the dead (those of the non-elect) lived not again until the thousand years were finished. This is the first*

> *resurrection (in which the souls of the elect, both the dead and the living, live and reign with Yahushua in the spiritual realm of the kingdom of God prior to the second coming). Blessed and holy is he that hath part in the first resurrection: on such the second death (soon to be explained) hath no power, but they shall be priests of God (Eloah) and of Christ (the Messiah), and shall reign with him a (figurative) thousand years. And when the thousand years are expired, Satan shall be loosed out of his prison, and shall go out to deceive the nations (think in terms of the prophecy of Matthew 24:24 concerning the great tribulation in which all the peoples of the world will be deceived, save those of the elect) which are in the four quarters of the earth, Gog and Magog, to gather them together to battle: the number of whom is as the sand of the sea. And they went up on the breadth of the earth, and compassed (surrounded) the camp of the saints about, and the beloved city (the city of new Jerusalem in heaven):* **and fire came down from God (Eloah) out of heaven, and devoured them. And the devil that deceived them was cast into the lake of fire and brimstone,** *where the beast and the false prophet are (from Revelation 19:20),* **and shall be tormented day and night for ever and ever.**" Revelation 20:5-10 (Parentheticals added for clarity; bold face added for emphasis)

In the second half of this passage, the rest of the non-elect who are still living after the first beast and the false prophet have been thrown into the burning lake of fire and brimstone and all the kings of the earth and their armies have been destroyed by the sword of Yahushua riding on His white horse, described in Revelation 19:21, face a similar fate to the kings of the earth and their armies: they will be destroyed by fire from God coming down from heaven. Immediately thereafter, the Apostle John describes the great white throne judgment before almighty God sitting on His throne in which all the people of the earth who have ever lived shall be judged by God for their actions done during their lives (for the non-elect) or based on the righteousness of Yahushua (for all those who numbered among God's elect and whose names are written in the Lamb's book of life) is reckoned or credited to us, and He has born the penalty for our sins by His sacrificial death on the cross in our place. Before this passage begins, all the non-elect, all of whom have died, will be raised from the dead, as Yahushua fully revealed and explained in John 5:28-30:

> *"Marvel not at this: for the hour is coming, in the which all that are in the graves (have died) shall hear his (the Son of God's) voice, And shall come forth; they that have done good (the elect), unto resurrection of life (at His second coming foretold in Matthew 24:30-31); and they that have done evil (after the conclusion of Revelation 20:9), unto the resurrection of damnation (soon to be described)."* (Parentheticals added for clarity)

Here is how the Apostle John describes the great white throne judgment of God:

> *"And I saw a great white throne, and him that sat on it (YHWH or God), from whose face the earth and heaven fled away (He is THAT fearsome and THAT worthy of our fear and awe!); and there was found no place for them (no place to run and nowhere to hide). And I saw the dead, small and great, stand before God (Eloah); and the book was opened, which is the (Lamb's) book of life: and the dead were judged out of those things which were written in the books, according to their works. And the sea gave up the dead which were in it; and death and hell delivered up the dead which were in them: and they were judged every man according to their works. And death and hell were cast into the lake of fire. This is the second death. And whosoever was not found written in the (Lamb's) book of life was cast into the lake of fire."* Revelation 20:11-15 (Parentheticals added for clarity)

Sprinkled throughout the Bible we see references to the Lamb's book of life which, from context, we can deduce is a book in heaven in which the names of all of YHWH's elect were written, before the foundation of the world, who would one day become Yahushua's born again elect followers and saints, who would give up or submit their lives to serve Him. Conversely, those whose names do not appear in this book of life, are those whom YHWH has created as the non-elect, those whom He has chosen to create as His vessels of dishonor, fitted unto His wrath and eventual damnation, as is described in Romans 9:21-23. All of the people whose names do not appear in the book of life are judged by their works during their lives, that are recorded in other books in heaven; and since all have sinned and fall short of the glory of God, all such people will be damned by YHWH at this great white throne judgment and cast into the lake of fire, where they will be tormented like the devil, the first beast and the false prophet, day and night for ever and ever.

I have written in *Making Sense Out of a World Gone Mad,* of a premonition I had of what I thought at the time was hell, which I now recognize to be the burning lake of fire and brimstone, which at the time I had never read of, and how absolutely terrifying and horrible that experience was for me, and would be for anyone. That premonition precisely matches the Bible's description of the lake of fire and brimstone in eternal torment, day and night without end. Clearly, God orchestrated all of that to get my attention, and He certainly did!

This passage and the teaching of Yahushua in John 5:28-30 from above reveals to us that every person who has ever lived will live forever in resurrected, immortal bodies: either enjoying eternal pleasures in paradise (heaven) with YHWH, Yahushua and all the other elect saints, or enduring unending torment in the burning lake of fire for having engaged in profound wickedness, foolishness and cruelty while in this life, that YHWH simply abhors and will not tolerate in His new heaven and new earth, wherein dwelleth righteousness, where there are no more lies and no more evil forever.

Ironically, YHWH's plan all along has been to direct a complete reversal of fortunes, so that those who were reviled by the world in this life, persecuted and abused for serving Yahushua (Christ), being of the truth and treating others with sacrificial love, will find ourselves inheriting lives of prosperity and profound joy and being entrusted by YHWH with significant responsibilities for stewarding a significant portion of God's kingdom for all eternity. This is what Yahushua meant when He taught that in the kingdom of God the first (in this life) shall be last (in the kingdom of God), and the last shall be first. Those of us who have been living our lives righteously in this life will finally reap our rewards for doing so in the life soon to come.

Similarly, those who lived lives of luxury, wealth, power and selfishness in this life, those who describe themselves as the elite, will find that what rewards they enjoyed in this life are all they will ever enjoy for the rest of eternity. So who gets the better deal, in the end? The answer is obvious: God's elect do, through no merit of our own. It is a gift from God so that He gets all the glory for it, for all eternity, which was His number one objective in His creating man and all of creation in the first place. Life was never all about us; it was always all about Him. Most of mankind has lived their entire lives getting everything 100% backwards! Only a rare few of us have been blessed enough to have YHWH and Yahushua reveal this full plan to us, so that we might live wise and sensible lives, which glorify God and bring kindness, blessings and wisdom to others. This, in the final analysis, is why we, the elect, were created by God in the first place.

The final scene of YHWH's play is described in Chapters 21 and 22 of Revelation, the last two chapters of the Bible, with an emphasis on describing the new heaven and new earth in a vision that John had, where we, the resurrected born again elect followers of YHWH and Yahushua, shall dwell for all eternity. It is well worth examining together the beginning of Chapter 21 that describes what most people refer to as heaven:

> *"And I saw a new heaven and a new earth:* **for the first heaven and the first earth were passed away**, *and there was no more sea. And I John saw the holy city, new Jerusalem, coming down from God (Eloah) out of heaven, prepared as a bride adorned for her husband. And I heard a great voice out of heaven saying, Behold, the tabernacle (tent or temple) of God (Eloah) is with men, and he will dwell with them, and they shall be his people, and God (Eloah) himself shall be with them, and be their God (Eloah). And God*

5. Is the Climax and Conclusion to YHWH's Play Now Just Around the Corner?

> *(Eloah) shall wipe away all tears from their eyes; and there shall be no more death, neither sorrow, nor crying, neither shall there be any more pain: for the former things are passed away. And he that sat upon the throne (YHWH) said, Behold, I make all things new. And he said unto me, Write: for these words are true and faithful. And he said unto me, It is done. I am Alpha and Omega, the beginning and the end. I will give to him that is athirst of the fountain of the water of life freely. He that overcometh shall inherit all things; and I will be his God (Eloah), and he shall be my son."* Revelation 21:1-7 (Parentheticals added for clarity)

This prophecy is simply amazing, when you think about it. First, YHWH is telling us that this earth will burn up or pass away and that we will live in a new Jerusalem, or new heaven and earth that YHWH has created for us to live in with Him in close proximity in an intimate sonship relationship. Second, He promises us that He will bring a permanent end to the sorrows and pain of our lives that for many of us have been very disheartening and painful to deal with. Third, He tells us that for those of us who hang in there, stand up to evil and lies when we encounter them, do not give up and overcome our adversaries, which YHWH promises us He will tread down for us in many places throughout the Book of Psalms, in particular, that we shall inherit that which is likely to vastly exceed anything that we can possibly imagine. In my own case, He has shown me in several visions recently that He intends for me to assume responsibility for a significant kingdom, over which He wishes for me to rule with the wisdom, knowledge and insight which I have acquired in my rather challenged life here, which He has given me. I am excited and thrilled at the prospect of being able to put my considerable gifts and talents to use for the benefit of others. It is a prospect which, quite frankly, exceeds my wildest expectations. But on what basis do I have to not believe Him? He has proven His reliability and trustworthiness to me repeatedly throughout my challenged life, especially over the last twenty years since I gave my life to Yahushua. So I have no reason not to believe and trust Him completely with respect to all of these promises.

In contrast to the promises which YHWH makes to His elect in the first seven verses of Chapter 21 of Revelation, He then makes a very interesting statement and promise concerning a group of people who will inevitably find themselves enduring torment in the burning lake of fire and brimstone. This is especially telling to us, right here at the end of God's play and it illustrates and demonstrates the total depravity of most of mankind in these final days of these end times. He tells us,

> ***"But the fearful, and unbelieving,*** *and the abominable, and murderers, and whoremongers, and sorcerers, and idolaters,* **and all liars**, *shall have their part in the lake which burneth with fire and brimstone: which is the second death."* Revelation 21:8 (Bold face added for emphasis)

These words define and describe well over 95% of humanity alive today in America and the world, do they not? Of course they do! In fact, I would submit to you that they describe well over 99% of all humanity alive on earth today, but I have chosen to work off of the lower number to make my point here. How is it that all the people wearing face diapers in public and complying with governmental and health authority mandates tied to the Covid hoax are not proving that they are fearful? Some may be fearful of contracting an upper respiratory infection diagnosed as Covid-19 that has a survival rate of some 99.76%. But most of the people complying with the mandates are far more fearful of being socially shamed for not complying with the mandates, in spite of the fact that honest science reveals that wearing face masks is materially harmful to the health of those wearing them and that social distancing and constant sanitizing are counter-productive to building herd immunity.[11] What we are witnessing is mass hysteria over an elaborate and sophisticated psychological operation and con job perpetrated upon the masses by our own

---

[11] See Appendix A for a well-reasoned, science-based explanation for why face masks should be avoided, from the book, *The Case Against Masks: Ten Reasons Why Mask Use Should be Limited,* by Judy A. Mikovits and Kent Heckenlively, JD.

governments to further enslave us and encroach on our legitimate freedoms to live our lives unhindered and unharrassed. The mass hysteria is being revealed by the widespread mask wearing in particular, that proves that the wearers have abandoned all independent research and critical thinking and succumbed to mass fear, that tells those of us who know what it all means what their fate is soon likely to be. It's as if they are advertising their own eternal damnation!

Almost our entire culture is unbelieving when it comes to YHWH, Yahushua and adherence to the entirety of the teachings of the KJV Bible. Most people I encounter are downright hostile to the Bible and willfully ignorant of the evidence supporting its reliability and inerrancy and the knowledge of how it was compiled and translated into English from the Hebrew and Greek manuscripts available to us.

As a man of honesty and impeccable intellectual integrity, it is my observation that at best one out of every 10,000 people is ***NOT*** a liar. There is nothing the least bit truthful about the Covid hoax and fraud and pretty much the same thing applies to the rampant denial of the truth that there is overwhelming and compelling evidence of rampant and egregious voter and election fraud in November's Presidential election. Perhaps fear of reprisals for speaking up and speaking out about the lawlessness is driving some people's unwillingness to do that which is right and to advance the lies of the demonic left and the mainstream media, but that just proves my earlier point over the epidemic of fearfulness and cowardice in our culture today. Either way, those manifesting such behaviors are advertising their own eternal damnation. It's just that simple.

The balance of the Book of Revelation describes this new heaven and new earth, the new Jerusalem, in further detail. The essence of all of it is that YHWH has planned to create a new home for His elect that promises to be far more amazing and wonderful than was the Garden of Eden described in the first three chapters of the Book of Genesis, and that YHWH and Yahushua will dwell therein with all of us saints (the elect) in harmony and peace. It's hard not to get excited at the prospect after the endless lies and tyrannical actions of the governments of the world over the Covid hoax and fraud this past year, isn't it?

Now, returning to where we are likely to be in YHWH's prophetic biblical timeline, we know that all prophecy, when fulfilled, is fulfilled perfectly and completely, as was demonstrated by the roughly 300 prophecies, roughly 60 of which were major ones, which were perfectly fulfilled by the life of Yahushua in His first advent. From Chapter 10 of *Making Sense Out of a World Gone Mad: A Roadmap for God's Elect Living in the Final Days of the End Times,* we now know that most of the seven seal, trumpet and vial judgments have already been poured out on earth during the last 1,900 years since the Book of Revelation was written by the Apostle John on the Isle of Patmos around 95 A.D.; but not everything. In particular, we are now seeing events converge in our world that appear to be on the brink of more completely fulfilling the prophecy of the mark of the beast and *"that no man might buy or sell, save he that had the mark, or the name of the beast, or the number of his name,"* which we know to be the number 666 (see Revelation 13:17-18).

In many places, we have witnessed public health and government authorities mandating the wearing of face masks in public places in response to the alleged Covid outbreak. Today in Europe and places such as the City of Los Angeles, businesses open to the public have been ordered closed due to recent upticks in reported Covid cases, which we now know to be highly manipulated and contrived, and mean next to nothing. But these mandates have the effect of barring all people, whether they are wearing masks or not, from buying and selling many items such as groceries, restaurant food and other goods and services. In other places, such as the rural mountain town in which I live, mask mandates are posted on all entrances to businesses open to the public, but they are not universally enforced; at least not yet. However, the first of at least three Covid vaccines has now obtained FDA approval for use and has begun to be distributed and administered to volunteers willing to take it. As Archbishop Viganò reports in his open letter to President Donald Trump, it appears that the plan of the global elites is to attempt to make the taking of one of the Covid vaccines universally mandatory for anyone who wishes to travel or to engage in commerce. As such, refusal to comply with a mandatory vaccine, if universally enforced, may result in a person being universally denied the right to buy or sell goods and services as described in Revelation 13:17, thereby completing the fulfillment of that as-yet-unfulfilled end times prophecy. [12]

I should add and acknowledge that Revelation 13:16 specifies that the mark of the beast is to be received in a person's right hand or in his forehead, which does not appear to describe either the mandatory wearing of a face mask or of receiving an injection of a Covid vaccine in one's arm. As with most of the Book of Revelation, verse 16 appears to be employing metaphorical language as it describes a person's allegiance or loyalty to the global political and economic beast system, as indicated by a person's obedience to or compliance with orders and mandates issued by the globalist beast system, in which a mark in the right hand signifies manual labor and a mark in the forehead signifies intellectual labor and service.

The Bible is silent on just how far the globalist beast system must take this mark of the beast tyranny and denial of our freedoms to engage in commerce. Perhaps it will be sufficient for it to be announced as universally mandatory and the penalties for non-compliance enumerated, or perhaps it will have to be implemented worldwide or in all places where God's elect reside; no one knows for certain, but it will be something we all should be watching closely for, because it will serve as yet another sign of where we are in YHWH's prophetic biblical timeline.

---

[12] See Appendix B for a science-based explanation for why these new vaccines should be avoided from a health perspective, over and above the likely and very serious spiritual implications of submitting to it.

Revelation 6:15-17 describes the rich and powerful of the world (the elites) hiding in the dens and rocks of the mountains from the wrath of "the face of him that sitteth on the throne (YHWH, or God) and from the wrath of the Lamb (Yahushua the Messiah)." These dens and rocks of the mountains certainly appear to be referring to the some 2,000 underground cities or Deep Underground Military Bases (DUMBs) worldwide (some 250 of them in the United States) that have been under construction since as early as the 1940s, ostensibly in the event of a nuclear war, but quite likely more in anticipation of the second coming of Yahushua. The $21 trillion that is unaccounted for from the Department of Defense (DOD) and Department of Housing and Urban Development (HUD) that Michigan State University Professor Mark Skidmore and his team of graduate students have uncovered since 2016, and which is now deemed a matter of national security that cannot be talked about (per FASAB Rule 56), is quite likely the financial consequence of these massive construction projects which have been underway in America and elsewhere for decades, that no one in government is the least bit interested in admitting to.

Many of us who research these sorts of things know that our government has concealed many advanced weaponry technologies from public knowledge. While the lying media reports from time to time of saber rattling between the United States and other nations such as China, Russia, North Korea and Iran, and the threat of war, it is far more likely that all of the leaders of the world, who report to the same puppet masters of the Illuminati and Freemasonry, are secretly preparing to join together and try to shoot Yahushua, or Christ, out of the sky upon His second coming. I fully grasp how utterly insane this both sounds and is, but what you must understand is that the world's global elites are desperate and will do virtually anything to try to avoid incurring the imminent fury and wrath of YHWH and Yahushua that the top leaders of the global conspiracy know is coming upon them, although they will never admit to it, and always need a cover to conceal and never reveal what they are really up to in secret.

5. Is the Climax and Conclusion to YHWH's Play Now Just Around the Corner?

When anyone thinks carefully about all of the theater and drama that we Americans have witnessed in our nation since 2016 in all the Trump bashing and false allegations made against Trump, including the fake Russia collusion narrative, the circus of the Brett Kavanaugh Supreme Court nomination hearing, followed by the totally unwarranted impeachment hearings, the Covid hoax, and the alleged race riots and violence over the death of George Floyd, allegedly at the hands of a white cop, a few of us realize that virtually everything we have witnessed over the last four years has to have been contrived and carefully scripted to bring about a total farce that makes no sense if you comprehend how the game of the rich and powerful is always played. What do I mean by this?

America is a nation of Hollywood illusions and con jobs from top to bottom. Nothing is what it appears to be and the charade between Donald Trump and his apparent opponents is no exception. It cannot possibly be anything else. The global elite beast system of Revelation 13:1-9 has known for decades that their global conspiracy, ruled and controlled by stealth and deception, cannot be beaten because they have carefully thought through and controlled all the reins of power for decades, if not centuries, worldwide. Their roadmap for global dominance was inadvertently revealed by the release of the *Protocols of the Learned Elders of Zion*, first in Russian in 1905, and then translated and first published in English in 1920. Anyone who has failed to read and understand the contents of this subversive book and plan is totally clueless how America and the rest of the world have been ruled by the rich and powerful Illuminati bloodline families for thousands of years. Their plan has been developed and refined over several centuries to slowly, gradually and with great patience usher in their New World Order from hell.

This globalist beast system operates in extreme secrecy and is highly compartmentalized so that only those at the very top of the secret society cabals of the occult know and understand the full plan. It is a many-headed hydra beast monster in which if you were to chop off one of its heads, three more would grow back in its place and this is all by careful design so that their plans cannot possibly be thwarted. Those who are high level members of the secret societies of Freemasonry, the Illuminati, the Jesuits, the Knights of Malta, the Knights of the Golden Dawn and many other interlocked secret societies all have sold their souls quite literally to the devil, in exchange for a few short years of wealth, fame, power and pleasures, and God has predestinated all of them to do just this to fulfill His sovereign plan of salvation for His elect.

Given all the false allegations that have been made against Trump by politicians on the political left, that have been fully colluded with by the FBI, the DOJ, the CIA and the lying Mockingbird mainstream media that has been directed by CIA operatives for decades, any critically thinking person would realize that the Marxist, demonic Democrat Party has been hell-bent on destroying America and American sovereignty any way they can over the last four years and that a majority of the American voters were likely to hand Donald Trump a landslide victory in November, which they did; although that is now in dispute because of widespread and egregious voter and election fraud which I predict will become widespread knowledge to the American public at some point.

Anyone directing the Democrat Party strategy to regain political power in the White House would have had to be grossly incompetent to direct the various members of the Democrat Party to engage in a campaign of demonizing and bearing false witness against Trump, all campaigns of which have failed miserably, unless this was their deliberate plan, which I believe it was. The manipulations that led to the selection of Joe Biden and Kamala Harris to head the Democrat Party ticket for President and Vice President and the serious liabilities and skeletons that these two mendacious politicians have in both of their closets, reveal yet again that the plan of The Powers That Be was to create the conditions that would lead to outright civil war in this country that would either lead to widespread death and destruction and the takeover of the American republic by a Marxist coup, or the imposition of some form of martial law that would serve as a pretext for the global elites to go hide in their underground bunkers and cities from the imminent second coming of Yahushua the Messiah that they know is coming, but will never admit to.

Today, two months after the November 3, 2020 election, the Mockingbird mainstream media perpetuates their endless denials that the Trump legal team has produced no tangible evidence of election fraud and they all are doing so in lockstep with one another. Meanwhile, the alternative media on the internet is abuzz with news of the extent and nature of the crimes that were committed by election and state government officials to steal the election from the American voters and from Donald Trump. All of what is being reported by the alternative media is highly credible and entirely consistent with my writings and teachings from the last six years, in which I have been asserting that all elections are corrupt and rigged. The evidence coming out now proves exactly how this election fraud has been accomplished to rig election outcomes between two morally deviant candidates for many decades. All that has changed this time around is that much of it is now out in the open for all those who want to know, see and hear about, and it should have the effect of generating righteous moral indignation and outrage directed at everyone who had to have known about or had a hand in this widespread and rampant fraud that makes a complete mockery of America's political systems and processes. As many political pundits and observers have noted recently, such overt fraud reveals that America's elections closely resemble those of a banana republic or a third world dictatorship and not what purports to be a constitutional republic governed by the rule of law and the leader of the so-called free world.

So far, Americans are living in one of two camps, and both are seething in anger directed at the other side. Those who identify themselves as Trump voters and supporters are outraged that the Democrat Party, the mainstream media, the FBI and DOJ and many state government officials and lower level courts have engaged in treachery, betrayal and in many cases outright treason, in concert with foreign governments (The Communist Party of the Chinese government being the most notable) to steal the election and the control of the American republic from them in a Communist coup and takeover. Those who identify themselves with the Democrat Party of the increasingly Communist left and who are, for whatever reason (most of it based on unfounded and unthinking emotion), strongly opposed to Donald Trump as President, are acting as though they believe that the Trump campaign's claims of fraud are totally unfounded, or they simply don't care: they just want their guy, Biden, to win and for Trump and his supporters to lose. While there is a well-defined process spelled out in the U.S. Constitution for how to resolve election disputes in Article II, Section 1, chances are that all parties this time around are going to try to duck the responsibility for resolving this dispute that has no winners and only losers and regardless of how they rule, is likely to erupt in widespread violence and hatred toward the other camp.

Having said all of this, let us not lose sight of the greater reality that I have been teaching in this book that God remains firmly in control on His throne in heaven and is orchestrating all of this rather troubling drama for His ultimate glory, honor, worship and praise. In light of this greater reality, has YHWH left us any clues as to how He might orchestrate the events which appear to be headed toward a monstrous collision in the very near future, especially as we realize that what motivates Him more than anything else is maximizing His glory? Thankfully, He has done just that in several stories told in the Old Testament. In all three instances in biblical history, YHWH has orchestrated amazing miracles and reversals of circumstances at the very last minute to save His people.

The first example of such a dramatic reversal occurs in Chapter 14 of the Book of Exodus in which the fleeing 12 Hebrew tribes led by Moses found themselves trapped on the shores of the Red Sea (the Gulf of Aqaba) as Pharaoh and his Egyptian army were barreling toward them in chariots and horses to slaughter the nation of Israel. All appeared lost and hopeless until, at the last moment, YHWH directed Moses to hold his staff over the waters and YHWH parted the Red Sea, the Hebrews fled across the dry land bridge which God had created, and once they were safely on the other side, God closed the waters and drowned Pharaoh and every last one of the pursuing Egyptian army. This rescue of God's people was a foreshadowing of many other instances in world history in which YHWH has done much the same thing that has had the effect of building the faith (trust) of His loyal followers to trust in and depend upon Him and Him alone.

In the Book of Esther, we have the story of Haman, the right hand lieutenant to the king of Babylon, King Ahasuerus, and Mordecai the Jew, who was the cousin of Queen Esther, in which Haman plotted to have Mordecai hung on a gallows that Haman ordered built for this purpose out of envy and spite toward Mordecai, and to have the Jews in the kingdom persecuted and killed. But through a series of circumstances, at the last minute, Queen Esther reveals the wicked plot to her husband the king, and the king has Haman hung on his own gallows and allows the Jews to round up and slaughter those in the kingdom who were conspiring to slaughter the Jews in his kingdom, which the Jews celebrate as the festival of Purim to this day.

In 2 Kings Chapters 6 and 7, we are told the story of the king of Syria who was besieging Samaria, the capital city of the northern kingdom of Israel, that created a great famine in the city that was so severe that some of the people were cannibalizing their own children to survive. So the king of Israel sent one of his aides to behead Elisha the prophet, because he had predicted these things in advance. But when the king's messenger arrived to kill Elisha, the prophet told the messenger that YHWH had told him that on the following day, food would be in abundance and that one measure of fine flour and two measures of barley would each be sold for a shekel in the gate of Samaria. That night, YHWH made the army of the Syrians hear the noise of chariots, horses and a great army and they assumed that the king of Israel had hired the kings and armies of his allies, the Hittites and the Egyptians, to come upon them and they all fled, leaving their tents, horses, silver, gold, clothing and food behind, that were discovered by four lepers who informed the king of Israel. Thus the people of Samaria ransacked the tents of the Syrians and sold the flour and the barley they came upon in the gate of Samaria the next day for the prices the prophet Elisha had predicted they would.

In all three stories mentioned here, YHWH brought about a dramatic reversal of fortunes at the very last minute. I suspect that YHWH has something similar in mind, at least for God's elect, at this time in world history, in which I expect that He will bring about a complete reversal of fortune that is likely to be so spectacular that I would not even venture to guess what it might be, because I know that my own ability to imagine such things is way too limited when it comes to the thoughts, ways and plans of brilliant and almighty God, YHWH.

What I think is quite likely is that YHWH will deliver on His promises concerning the ultimate fate of the wicked and the foolish of this corrupt and wicked world, which we can see repeated in many places in the Book of Psalms. Here are just a few of those passages which YHWH has inspired:

> *"Let all mine enemies be ashamed and sore vexed: let them return and be ashamed* ***suddenly****."* Psalm 6:10 (Bold face added for emphasis)

> *"Behold, he (the wicked) travaileth with iniquity, and hath conceived mischief, and brought forth falsehood. He made a pit, and digged it, and is fallen into the ditch which he made. His mischief shall return upon his own head, and his violent dealing shall come down upon his own pate."* Psalm 7:14-16

> *"The heathen are sunk down in the pit that they made: in the net which they hid is their own foot taken. The LORD (YHWH) is known by the judgment which he executeth: the wicked is snared in the work of his own hands. Higgaion. Selah."* Psalm 9:15-16

> *"The LORD (YHWH) trieth the righteous: but the wicked and him that loveth violence his soul hateth. Upon the wicked shall he rain snares, fire and brimstone, and an horrible*

> *tempest: this shall be the portion of their cup. For the righteous LORD (YHWH) loveth righteousness; his countenance doth behold the upright."* Psalm 11:5-7

> *"The LORD (YHWH) shall cut off all flattering lips, and the tongue which speaketh proud things."* Psalm 12:3

> *"Let them be confounded and put to shame that seek after my soul: let them be turned back and brought to confusion that devise my hurt. Let them be as chaff before the wind: and let the angel of the LORD (YHWH) chase them. Let their way be dark and slippery: and let the angel of the LORD (YHWH) persecute them. For without cause they hid for me their net in a pit, which without cause they have digged for my soul. Let destruction come upon him at unawares; and let his net that he hath hid catch himself: into that very destruction let him fall."* Psalm 35:4-8

> *"As the fire burneth a wood, and as the flame setteth the mountains on fire; So persecute them with thy tempest, and make them afraid with thy storm. Fill their faces with shame; that they may seek thy name, O LORD (YHWH). Let them be confounded and troubled for ever; yea, let them be put to shame, and perish: That men may know that thou, whose name alone is JEHOVAH (Yahuwah or YHWH), art the most high over all the earth."* Psalm 83:14-16

> *"And he shall bring upon them their own iniquity, and cut them off in their own wickedness; yea, the LORD (YHWH) our God (Elohim) shall cut them off."* Psalm 94:23

> *"Let mine adversaries be clothed with shame, and let them cover themselves with their own confusion, as with a mantle."* Psalm 109:29

So the common themes of exposing, shaming and disgracing the wicked, their being confused and confounded, and their falling into the very traps which they have set to trap and harm the righteous keep coming up again and again in the Book of Psalms in which the psalmists are crying out to YHWH for relief and justice. These now appear to be the ultimate outcomes of the great Covid scam, the Great Reset (of the World Economic Forum) and the great election fraud of 2020, that I suspect none of the perpetrators of these crimes against humanity, nor their useful idiot followers, can begin to see or grasp. Here, in a nutshell is the imminent end of all of them:

> *"He that soweth iniquity shall reap vanity; and the rod of his anger shall fail."* Proverbs 22:8

The complete reversal that I am anticipating in the very near future is likely to be a huge surprise to virtually everyone, including those of us of the elect. So get your popcorn, grab a seat and enjoy the show! I'm expecting some real fireworks, and very dramatic surprises and you should be too!

6. YHWH's Lessons of Life Wisdom to His Elect

At the outset of this book, I revealed that Moses had told us in Psalm 90:9-10 that all of life is a stage and that we are merely actors on it for a short while and then we pass away and are no more, at least in this temporal life. The conclusion to Psalm 90 reveals what the entirety of this play has really been all about all along. Read it very carefully:

> *"Who knoweth the power of thine anger? even according to they fear, so is thy wrath.* **So teach us to number our days, that we may apply our heart unto wisdom.** *Return, O LORD (YHWH), how long? and let it repent thee concerning thy servants. O satisfy us early with thy mercy; that we may rejoice and be glad all our days. Make us glad according to the days wherein thou hast afflicted us, and the years wherein we have seen evil. Let thy work appear unto thy servants, and thy glory unto their children. And let the beauty of the LORD (YHWH) our God (Elohim) be upon us; yea, the work of our hands establish thou it."* Psalm 90:11-17 (Bold face added for emphasis)

This is the perspective from one of YHWH's most godly and faithful prophets who has spent more time with God on this earth than perhaps any other prophet, save Yahushua Himself. That is why I believe we should read and meditate upon these words very carefully because they offer those of us of the elect deep insight into what all of life is, and really has been, all about. So this is the insight and perspective of the godly and very wise. This stands in contrast and sharp relief to the view of life held by the vast majority of humanity who has ever lived throughout the last 6000 years of world history, as told through the words of Sir Francis Bacon, the unacknowledged son of Queen Elizabeth I of England, a founder of the Order of the Rose Cross or the Rosicrucians, a leader of Freemasonry and likely the real author of the play, *Macbeth*, which appears to be falsely attributed to William Shakespeare, for reasons of political convenience and the concealment of its real author: [13]

> "Life is a tale, told by an idiot, full of sound and fury, signifying nothing." [14]

So what we see here is the very sharp contrast between the understanding, wisdom and insight of the prophet Moses, author of the first five books of the Bible and a paragon of godly virtue, who clearly knew God intimately and personally as one of His elect, and the very worldly and ungodly Sir Francis Bacon, who serves as the prototype of all of the non-elect: the wicked and the foolish, bound for eternal torment in the burning lake of fire and brimstone, for having rejected God and pursued a life of selfishness and hedonism, rooted in this rather pathetic outlook on the purpose and meaning of life; namely, that there is none. For the wicked and the foolish, the notion of a life having purpose and meaning is incomprehensible to them, and this explains their reckless and self-absorbed ways in which they live their entire lives. As such, this life philosophy becomes a self-fulfilling prophecy for them, which defines reckless folly.

Today, the vast majority of the world sits on a precipice about to plunge to its demise below, due to its own recklessness and folly. Led by leaders, both covert and their more public puppets, these self-appointed elites have lived Sir Francis Bacon's life philosophy with abandon and gusto. And what has it gotten them in the end? Only a few of us, the elect, can see clearly enough to realize that it is on the brink of bringing them confusion, public shame and disgrace and their eternal

---

[13] Sora, Steven. *Rosicruican America: How a Secret Society Influenced the Destiny of a Nation.* pp 41-43.

[14] www.goodreads.com/quotes/8232323-life-is-a-tale-told-by-an-idiot-full-of.

destruction. Was it the least bit worth it in the end? I should say not, but you will never convince any of them of this.

But for a small remnant of us, the conclusion to God's story, as told in the Bible from beginning to end, drives home and teaches us that without the truth of God and without the testimonies, precepts, laws, statutes and teachings of His word and of His acts in history in the affairs of men, we too would be lost and damned forever and that our lives would have been meaningless and wasted as well. Thankfully, our lives have not been meaningless, they were not wasted and the best is yet to come.

YHWH has quite intentionally created a world of illusions and deceptions in which He has deposited all of us. And then, for a small few, He chooses to reveal the truth to us. Here is how He puts it:

> *It is the glory of God (Elohim) to conceal a thing: but the honour of kings is to search out a matter."* Proverbs 25:2

These revelations are so profound and so shocking, that they transform us forever and from that moment on, the world has no hold on us. We live in it, but we are no longer of it. We have abandoned the shiny lures and distracting attractions of an illusory world for eternal truth, righteousness, nobility, kindness and true courage that can only be found in total submission and surrender to a sovereign, all-knowing, all-powerful and brilliant God who has nothing but our best long-term interests at heart. We are investing our lives for the long-term, in the eternal. As such, the attractions of money, power, fame, status, popularity and the approval of those who are wicked fools means nothing to us, because we know it is all passing away and perishing. As long as we enjoy the approval and delight of our divine Father, YHWH, whom admittedly we cannot see, but who makes His presence felt in our lives in many undeniable but private ways, none of the rest of it matters and has no value to how we invest our lives in others.

Simply put, YHWH is a God of truth in a world ruled by His created spirit being, Satan, the prince of this world, the father of lies and the destroyer. The KJV Bible, every word of which was inspired by YHWH, is 100% trustworthy, reliable and true. Nothing else is. Anything which contradicts or conflicts with it in any way is, by definition, a lie and all lies find their origin in the devil, the father of lies. The most effective lie ever told is that the devil, the enemy of all of mankind, does not even exist. Nothing could be further from the truth. Anyone who fails to embrace the wisdom and truths contained in this paragraph, is a blind fool and a danger to himself and to anyone entrusted to his care. I cannot be more emphatic on this.

This wisdom comes from a lifetime of pain lived out trying to bring delight to God in a world which hates Him with an unbridled passion, because He did not choose them, whereas He chose me, through no merit of my own. It was all by His grace and mercy alone, which He chose to bless me with, for which I am eternally grateful and humbled beyond words for His many blessings, none of which I deserve. But because of whose I am, the world hates me for it, just as Yahushua promised us would happen. I fully get it and I accept it. I don't like it, but I would not have grown in wisdom and knowledge, had I liked everything YHWH chose to confront me with to chasten, instruct and refine me into the man I have become today. I have no regrets. YHWH knew fully what He was doing, although I often did not at the time He was allowing various afflictions to beset me.

The world is ruled by pathological liars, thieves, con artists and psychopaths. Many other people live their entire lives playing fast and loose with the truth and thinking that they are getting away with their trickery and dishonesty. They think they are so clever and that they have pulled one over on God. They haven't. God sees and is recording it all in His books in heaven and nothing surprises Him because after all, He predestinated everything. If this reality is not obvious to you by now, you haven't been paying attention to the clues and evidence of this all around you. This is no accident.

YHWH reveals in His word, the KJV Bible, that all men are born depraved, selfish, sinful liars, separated from a right relationship with Him and bound for hell when we die. No one is good; no, not one. So put that notion out of your mind forever. We are all born to lose, and most of us die proving it. That's just a fact. You may not like it. But that in no way changes objective, absolute, universal reality.

A wise person stops being offended by the the truth and faces it and its implications head on and deals with them responsibly, as I have. I know it can be done, because I have done it, by God's grace and the power of His Holy Spirit living in and working through me. Is it hard? Sure it's hard! Nothing worth attaining comes easy, so put that notion out of your mind forever. That which is hard builds character when you overcome it. And having a character of honesty, integrity, courage, virtue, wisdom, knowledge, courage, fear of God and selflessness is worth far more than great wealth in the kingdom of God, where we are heading. Everything in this life has been a testing and proving ground for both the elect and the non-elect. Nothing surprises YHWH because He created each of us uniquely as He planned from the beginning. If this is too hard for you to wrap your head around, get over it. He's God and you're not, remember?

Those of us of the elect are heading to a new heaven and new earth wherein dwelleth righteousness, in which we will become heirs to YHWH, and based on what He has predestinated for each of us, we will inherit certain rewards and responsibilities. In my own case, I fully trust YHWH to know what is best for me and for Him, so I don't dwell on thinking about such things at all. My relationship with Him of total trust, confidence and devotion frees me from having to even think about such matters. But I am eager to assume significant responsibilities to care responsibly for whatever portion of God's kingdom He chooses to entrust to my care and He knows with total confidence what I am and am not capable of handling and He knows I will speak up, if I have my own doubts. That's the kind of relationship of absolute integrity we have between us today.

In many places in God's word, we are taught to fear God and keep His commandments. I think Solomon says it most succinctly when he teaches us,

> *"Let us hear the conclusion of the whole matter:* **Fear God (Elohim), and keep his commandments:** *for this is the whole duty of man."* Ecclesiastes 12:13 (Bold face added for emphasis)

Many modern day con artists who play fast and loose with the truth and are foolish enough to contradict Solomon, one of the wisest men who ever lived, falsely claim that God is love and that's all you have to know. Implicitly they are trying to suggest that God is an indulgent and not-too-bright pushover who can be easily conned, and need not be feared or obeyed. But Yahushua Himself claims precisely the opposite, and in so doing, reveals these frauds and charlatans for what they clearly are:

> *"And fear not them which kill the body, but are not able to kill the soul:* **but rather fear him (YHWH) which is able to destroy both soul and body in hell.***"* Matthew 10:28 (Bold face added for emphasis)

Furthermore, the Bible is crystal clear that the fear of God is the prerequisite to all knowledge, wisdom and understanding:

> *"The* **fear of the LORD (YHWH) is the beginning of knowledge**: *but fools despise wisdom and instruction."* Proverbs 1:7 (Bold face added for emphasis)

> *"My son, if thou wilt receive my words, and hide my commandments with thee; so that thou incline thine ear unto wisdom, and apply thine heart to understanding: Yea if thou criest after knowledge, and liftest up thy voice for understanding; If thou seekest her as silver, and searchest for her as hid treasures;* **Then shalt thou understand the fear of the LORD (YHWH), and find the knowledge of God (Elohim).** *For the LORD (YHWH) giveth wisdom: out of his mouth cometh knowledge and understanding. He layeth up sound wisdom for the righteous: he is a buckler (shield) to them that walk uprightly. He keepeth the paths of judgment (doing the right thing), and preserveth the way of his saints. Then shalt thou understand righteousness and judgment, and equity (fairness); yea, every good path. When wisdom entereth into thine heart, and knowledge is pleasant to*

> *thy soul; Discretion shall preserve thee, understanding shall keep thee:"* Proverbs 2:1-11 (Parentheticals added for clarity; bold face added for emphasis)

> ***"Be not wise in thine own eyes: fear the LORD (YHWH) and depart from evil."*** Proverbs 3:7 (Bold face added for emphasis)

Similarly, these and other charlatans who claim to be followers of Christ play games with which commandments they choose to obey and which ones they defy. Many forms of evangelical or Protestant denominational organized religion sanction women pastors, elders and deacons, which a simple and honest reading of 1 Timothy 2:11-15 and chapter 3 clearly forbid. And inevitably, as soon as they tolerate such overt rebellion against God's commandments, their teachings depart materially from the teachings of the entirety of the Bible and make a mockery of anything resembling honesty, intellectual or moral integrity, or anything of God.

In order to keep all of God's commandments, to do His will, the godly person walking in integrity must seek out the entire word of God to see and know what it says and not rely on anyone else to tell him or her what's in there and what's not. This means that the faithful follower of Yahushua devotes him or herself to reading the KJV Bible from beginning to end virtually continuously. For example, I am now working on my eighth full reading of the Bible, reading three chapters from the Old Testament and three chapters from the New Testament every day. This usually takes me about an hour a day, but it is time well spent and even on my eighth read of it, I am discovering new insights, as I do each time I read it, which strengthens and deepens my relationship with and appreciation for YHWH and Yahushua.

Reading, contemplating upon and obeying God's word increasingly and profoundly changes those of us who do these things:

> *"And be not conformed to this world (of lies and evil):* **but be ye transformed by the renewing of your mind,** *that ye may prove what is that good, and acceptable, and perfect, will*

> *of God (Eloah)."* Romans 12:2 (Parenthetical added for clarity; bold face added for emphasis)

Finally, if one is reading and obeying God's word and commandments faithfully, he cannot help but discover that YHWH is the God of truth, that Yahushua came to testify to the truth and that only those who are of the truth hear His voice:

> *"Into thine hand I commit my spirit: thou hast redeemed me,* ***O LORD (YHWH) God (El) of truth.****"* Psalm 31:5 (Bold face added for emphasis)

> *". . . To this end was I born, and for this cause came I into the world,* **that I should bear witness unto the truth. Everyone that is of the truth heareth my voice** *(and conversely, everyone that is of the lie, does not hear His voice)."* John 18:37 (Parenthetical added for clarity; bold face added for emphasis)

> *"Jesus (Yahushua) saith unto him,* ***I am*** *the way,* ***the truth****, and the life: no man cometh unto the Father, but by me."* John 14:6 (Bold face added for emphasis)

This distinction between truth and lies is vitally important and seldom emphasized or given the attention it warrants among those professing to be Christians or followers of Yahushua. Anyone who lies or plays word games to distort the truth of God's word and His intent is revealing himself to be a fraud and tool of the devil, the father of lies and the destroyer, and not at all who or what he claims to be. Beware of wolves in sheep's clothing! For they are everywhere today!

Here is how the Apostle Peter summarizes the whole purpose of man and where we now find ourselves within YHWH's prophetic and biblical timeline:

> *"But the day of the Lord will come as a thief in the night (meaning unannounced and by surprise); in the which the heavens shall pass away with a great noise,* **and the elements shall melt with fervent heat, the earth also and the works that are therein shall be burned up**. *Seeing then that all these things shall be*

> *dissolved, what manner of persons ought ye to be in all holy conversation and godliness, Looking for and hasting unto the coming of the day of God (Eloah), wherein the heavens being on fire shall be dissolved, and the elements shall melt with fervent heat? Nevertheless we, according to his promise, look for new heavens and a new earth, wherein dwelleth righteousness. Wherefore, beloved, seeing that ye look for such things, be diligent that ye may be found of him in peace, without spot, and blameless."* 2 Peter 3:10-14 (Parenthetical added for clarity; bold face added for emphasis)

I cannot think of a more fitting end to God's story and this end to the final act of His play; can you?

Appendices

Appendix A, which follows, summarizes the overwhelming and compelling scientific evidence and reasoning for why the use of face masks should be strictly limited, rather than made a ubiquitous mandate and requirement for public life that has many overtones and suggestions of the mark of the beast of Revelation 13 and elsewhere.

Appendix B offers medical evidence and reasoning for why the mRNA Covid-19 vaccine, which is now available and being offered to people, should be avoided for health reasons and because of all the uncertainty surrounding their safety, from a lifelong health care practioner. As with the mask mandates, the globalist beast system is using its mass media to frighten many people into submitting to these new, unproven and potentially quite harmful vaccines for which the pharmaceutical industry bears effectively no legal liability for adverse health reactions to their products which appear to have been unwisely rushed to market in 2020.

For readers wishing to learn more about the risks of the new Covid-19 vaccines, here is a 28 minute video featuring some 20-30 experienced healthcare providers offering their concerns regarding the dangers of these new and unproven vaccines:

https://brandnewtube.com/v/75grLS

Appendix A

The Case Against Masks: Ten Reasons why Mask Use Should be Limited by Dr. Judy A. Mikovits and Kent Heckenlively, JD [15]

1. Human beings breathe oxygen and exhale carbon dioxide. Oxygen is 20.9% of the air we breathe in, but only 16% of what we breathe out. OSHA regulations state than any oxygen level below 19.5% is dangerous. Carbon dioxide makes up only 0.04% of the atmosphere, but 4% of the air we exhale (a 100-fold increase). Carbon dioxide toxicity begins at a level around 10%. Masks lower oxygen levels and raise carbon dioxide levels.
2. SARS-CoV-2 (Covid-19) spreads mainly through respiratory droplets from infected individuals who are coughing, hacking or sneezing and in close sustained contact with others. It does not appear to spread through regular breathing from people in typical social interactions.
3. Masks have varying degrees of effectiveness, but the more effective they are at blocking air flow, the lower your oxygen levels, and the higher the carbon dioxide levels, will be. Studies have shown that masks raise complaints of shortness of breath, headaches, and dizziness, suggesting lower oxygen and higher carbon dioxide levels.
4. You do not need to be six feet apart from a person *and* wearing a mask. The WHO does not recommend a six-foot distance for social distancing, but only a three-foot distance. Reputable publications such as *The Lancet* have reported that there is "scarce" evidence that masks provide effective protection against respiratory infections (Covid-19 is a form of respiratory infection).
5. Masks disrupt normal patterns of air flow, leading to pathogens being deposited on chins, cheeks and near eyes. A small study from South Korea showed that

[15] From the book by the same name by the same authors, published in 2020, pp. 75-77.

Covid-19 easily passed through several different types of masks.

6. Unless you are close to someone who is singing or speaking very loudly, such as in a choir, the risk of airborne transmission is very low, especially since it is difficult for coughing people to sing. Super-spreader events have appeared to have taken place only in indoor events and among individuals in prolonged and intimate contact with each other, singing or talking loudly. Sunlight is a potent killer of this virus, often destroying it within a few minutes.

7. Nursing homes are dangerous for spreading SARS-CoV-2, as residents of nursing homes normally have lowered immunity. The lowered immunity makes them most susceptible to developing Covid-19 from exposure to SARS-CoV-2. Reports indicate that 42% of Covid-19 cases (whose diagnosis is often highly suspect) have come through nursing homes, which account for only 0.6% of the population. Recent data from several states suggest that number might be substantially higher. Having heart disease, diabetes, or chronic lung disease also increases your chances of disease from any upper respiratory infection.

8. Masks can become virus traps, leading to increased chances for infection when you touch the masks with your hands. The CDC has abundantly documented how well viruses can remain active on N95 respirator masks, and there is no reason to believe the results would not be the same for other types of masks.

9. There is no such thing as an "asymptomatic" carrier (as is repeatedly claimed by the lying media), who is alleged to have the virus without symptoms for weeks, months, or years. The *New England Journal of Medicine* recently published an article from several researchers claiming that wearing a mask outside of a health care facility "offers little, if any, protection from infection." This becomes all

the more absurd and unwarranted when the mortality rate from Covid-19 is reported to be 0.24%.

10. Children should return to school in the fall (of 2020) without masks. Multiple studies and infection patterns indicate that children are less likely to get infected, and when they are infected they have more mild symptoms (and thus are less likely to be coughing and hacking) and do not spread the virus to teachers, parents, or grandparents.

Author's note: I contracted a persistent upper respiratory infection from daily mask use during the summer of 2020 driving buses for the rafting industry in Jackson, WY. It was not bacterial; it was either due to a virus, fungi or other form of pathogen. Thus, a five-day course of azithromycin (a Z Pack) had no effect. Under the care of my holistic healthcare practioner, I took a 30-day supply of a Natural Z-Pak containing a number of substances known to enhance one's immune system, received multiple injections of ozone gas into both my nostrils, consumed garlic and honey five times a day and scattered cut onion halves throughout my living quarters to kill any pathogens I was being exposed to and to enhance my immune system. It took roughly a month to recover from it. Had I not been required to wear a face mask for my employment six days a week, I seriously doubt I would have had to contend with this infection. What astounds me is that almost no one talks about enhancing herd and individual immunity from a respiratory infection that is no more deadly that the annual flu.

Clearly, mask wearing mandates have nothing to do with protecting public health and everything to do with pursuing a political agenda to enslave the masses and secure their compliance with whatever government officials tell them to do, regardless of what the real science tells any thinking person who seeks to inform himself of the facts.

Appendix B

Covid Vaccine Information Letter to Patients

December 2020

Patients and Friends,

Last week I must have been asked 20 times about the new COVID vaccines. Here are my thoughts. Please pass this information on to as many as you can. People need to have fully informed consent when it comes to injecting foreign genetic material into their bodies.

1. The COVID vaccines are mRNA (meaning messenger RNA) vaccines. mRNA vaccines are a completely new type of vaccine. No mRNA vaccine has ever been licensed for human use before. In essence, we have absolutely no idea what to expect from this vaccine. We have no idea if it will be effective or safe.

2. Traditional vaccines simply introduce pieces of a virus to stimulate an immune reaction. The new mRNA vaccine is completely different. It actually injects (transfects) molecules of synthetic genetic material from non-human sources into our cells. Once in the cells, the genetic material interacts with our transfer RNA (tRNA) to make a foreign protein that supposedly teaches the body to destroy the virus being coded for. Note that these newly created proteins are not regulated by our own DNA, and are thus completely foreign to our cells. What they are fully capable of doing is unknown.

3. The mRNA molecule is vulnerable to destruction. So, in order to protect the fragile mRNA strands while they are being inserted into our DNA, they are coated with PEGylated lipid nanoparticles. This coating hides the mRNA from our immune system which ordinarily would kill any foreign material injected into the body. PEGylated lipid nanoparticles have been used in several different drugs for years. Because of their effect on immune system balance, several studies have shown them to induce allergies and autoimmune diseases. Additionally, PEGylated lipid nanoparticles have been shown to trigger

their own immune reactions, and to cause damage to the liver.

4. These new vaccines are additionally contaminated with aluminum, mercury, and possibly formaldehyde. The manufacturers have not yet disclosed what other toxins they contain.

5. Since viruses mutate frequently, the chance of any vaccine working for more than a year is unlikely. That is why the flu vaccine changes every year. Last year's vaccine is no more valuable than last year's newspaper.

6. Absolutely no long-term safety studies have been done to ensure that any of these vaccines don't cause cancer, seizures, heart disease, allergies, and autoimmune diseases seen with other vaccines. If you ever wanted to be a guinea pig for Big Pharma, now is your golden opportunity.

7. Many experts question whether the mRNA technology is ready for prime time. In November 2020, Dr. Peter Jay Hotez said of the new mRNA vaccines, "I worry about innovation at the expense of practicality because they [the mRNA vaccines] are weighted toward technology platforms that have never made it to licensure before." Dr. Hotez is Professor of Pediatrics and Molecular Virology & Microbiology at Baylor College of Medicine, where he is also Director of the Children's Hospital Center for Vaccine Development.

8. Michal Linial, PhD is a professor of Biochemistry. Because of her research and forecasts on COVID-19, Dr. Linial has been widely quoted in the media. She recently stated, "I won't be taking it [the mRNA vaccine] immediately - probably not for at least the coming year. We have to wait and see whether it really works. We will have a safety profile for only a certain number of months, so if there is a long-term effect after two years, we cannot know."

9. In November 2020, The Washington Post reported on hesitancy among healthcare professionals in the United States to the mRNA vaccines, citing surveys which reported that: "some did not want to be in the first round, so they could wait and see if there are potential side effects," and that "doctors and nurses want more data before championing vaccines to end the pandemic."
10. Since the death rate from COVID resumed to the normal flu death rate way back in early September, the pandemic has been over since then. Therefore, at this point in time no vaccine is needed. The current scare tactics regarding "escalating cases" are based on a PCR test that because it exceeds 34 amplifications has a 100% false positive rate unless it is performed between the 3rd and 5th day after the first day of symptoms. It is therefore 100% inaccurate in people with no symptoms. This is well established in the scientific literature.
11. The other reason you don't need a vaccine for COVID-19 is that substantial herd immunity has already taken place in the United States. This is the primary reason for the end of the pandemic.
12. Unfortunately, you cannot completely trust what you hear from the media. They have consistently got it wrong for the past year. Since they are all supported by Big Pharma and the other entities selling the COVID vaccines, they are not going to be fully forthcoming when it comes to mRNA vaccines. Every statement I have made here is fully backed by published scientific references.
13. I would be very interested to see verification that Bill and Melinda Gates with their entire family including grandchildren, Joe Biden and President Trump and their entire families, and Anthony Fauci and his entire family all get the vaccine.
14. Anyone who after reading all this still wants to get injected with the mRNA vaccine, should at the very least have their blood checked for COVID-19 antibodies.

> There is no need for a vaccine in persons already naturally immunized.

Here's my bottom line: I would much rather get a COVID infection than get a COVID vaccine. That would be safer and more effective. I have had a number of COVID positive flu cases this year. Some were old and had health concerns. Every single one has done really well with natural therapies including ozone therapy and IV vitamin C. Just because modern medicine has no effective treatment for viral infections, doesn't mean that there isn't one.

Yours always,

Frank Shallenberger, MD, HMD [16]

---

[16] Dr. Frank Shallenberger practices medicine and runs the Nevada Center for Alternative and Anti-Aging Medicine in Carson City, Nevada.

Bibliography

Bennett, Todd D. *Names: The Father, the Son and the Importance of Names in Scriptures.* Shema Yisrael Publications, New York, NY, 2006. ISBN: 0-9768659-2-0.

Mikovits, Dr. Judy A. and Heckenlively, Kent, JD. *Plague of Corruption: Restoring Faith in the Promise of Science.* Skyhorse Publishing, New York, NY, 2020. ISBN: 978-1-5107-5224-5

Mikovits, Dr. Judy A. and Heckenlively, Kent, JD. *The Case Against Masks: Ten Reasons Why Mask use Should be Limited.* Skyhorse Publishing, New York, NY, 2020. ISBN: 978-1-5107-6429-3

Perloff, James. *COVID-19 Red-Pilled: and the Agendas to Come.* Refuge Books, Burlington, MA, 2020. ISBN: 978-0-9668160-4-4

Protocols of the Meetings of the Learned Elders of Zion. Pyramid Book Shop, Houston, TX, 1934 (first published in Russian in 1905). ISBN: 978-1-162935133.

Schwab, Klaus and Malleret, Thierry. *COVID-19: The Great Reset.* World Economic Forum, Geneva, Switzerland, 2020. ISBN: 978-2-940631-12-4

Sora, Steven. *Rosicrucian America: How a Secret Society Influenced the Destiny of a Nation.* Destiny Books, Rochester, VT, 2019. ISBN: 978-1-62055-906-2

The Constitution of the United States. National Center for Constitutional Studies, USA, 2016. ISBN: 978-0-88080-144-7

The Hebraic-Roots Version Scriptures. Institute for Scripture Research, Republic of South Africa, 2004. ISBN: 0-9584353-9-1.

VAXXED: From Cover-up to Catastrophe. Cinema Libre Studio, USA, 2016.

About the Author

Watchman on the Wall is a researcher, author and blogger on the global conspiracy and its obvious connections to the fulfillment of end times Bible prophecy, what it all means and what we can expect in the very near future.

Prior to his current career, Watchman was a business management consultant and turnaround Chief Financial Officer (CFO) and general manager for half a dozen smaller high and low tech companies in the San Francisco Bay Area over a 30 year career in a variety of challenging conditions. He was instrumental in the successful turnaround and sale of one of those companies in a mergers & acquisitions transaction and in turning around and taking a second company public in an Initial Public Offering (IPO) and remained as that company's public company CFO for five years thereafter.

Watchman holds a bachelor's degree in Economics from U.C. Davis with Highest Honors and Phi Beta Kappa and Phi Kappa Phi honors distinctions and an MBA degree from the Harvard Business School with second year honors. As part of his formal education and subsequent research on his own, he has a particular expertise in and understanding of world history, political science, economics, philosophy, psychology, finance, business strategy, organizational behavior, American sociology and biblical theology, all of which were instrumental in the writing of his books.

For More Writings by the Author

Watchman on the Wall has authored the following ground-breaking books:

> *Making Sense Out of World Gone Mad: A Roadmap for God's Elect Living in the Finals Days of the End Times,* (published in February 2015)
>
> *Spiritual Warfare in the Final Days of the End Times* (published in September 2016)
>
> *Reflections of a Watchman on the Wall in the Final Days of the End Times* (published in October 2016)

More recently, he has authored:

> *The Final Act of God's Play* (published in January 2021)
>
> *The Great Con: Solving the Mystery of Trump and Q Anon* (published in March 2021)

He is now authoring the following three books simultaneously in 2021:

> *COVID-19: The Great Psyop*
>
> *The Emasculation of Men: How it is done, Who is behind it and What can be done about it*
>
> *Solving the Jewish Question*

The author has extensively blogged under his Watchman on the Wall moniker on Disqus and maintains his own website and blog at:

http://www.awatchmanonthewall.com

Made in the USA
Middletown, DE
29 August 2021